The United States no one is talking About

Clifton Bryant Jr.

ISBN 978-1-957582-65-8 (paperback)
ISBN 978-1-957582-66-5 (hardcover)
ISBN 978-1-957582-67-2 (digital)

Printed in the United States of America

Preface

This country has 34 million people living in poverty, with the numbers increasing due to the number of people who lost their jobs due to the Covid-19 Pandemic.

1. Jessica Semega, Melissa Kollar, Emily A Shrider, and John Creamer, "Income, Poverty in the United States: 2019", United Census Bureau, September 15, 2020, https://www.census.gov/library/publications/2020/demo/p60-270.html.

During the 2020 Presidential election, not one of the presidential candidates, the social media, news affiliates, and anyone in authority to speak up about our national disgrace: the neglect of our own while helping other countries in need.

The need for social welfare reform such as increases in Social Security Insurance benefits, Women, infants, and children (WIC), Supplemental Nutrition Assistance Program (SNAP), also formerly known as the Food Stamp Program, and the Affordable Care Act (ACA). Also, fair and equitable housing, the diversion of Foreign Aid funding to fix our impoverished communities, and the real reasons why crimes exist. It was prevalent that these topics that referenced the quality of life of the working poor would never be the focal point of discussion because it would involve taking from the wealthy and giving to those who made them rich; the poor.

Even with President Biden increasing the food stamps in the amount of 1 billion, which sounds like a lot until you do the math and realize each recipient would receive an extra $36.00 per month. For the working poor, this is enough to keep a person continuously looking for a "handout." American can do better in taking care of its own.

2. Tami Luhby, "Biden is about to send $1 billion more in food stamps to the 25 million neediest Americans, CNN.com, April 2, 2021, (https://www.cnn.com/2021/04/02/politics/food-stamps-hunger-americans-relief/index.html).

I wrote this book to appeal to the new administration to look at the issues neglected by the previous Administrations, to give those living in impoverishment a fighting chance to escape poverty. To make America a great nation by meeting the needs of everyone!

Qualifications

I grew up in poverty. I am the 2nd child of a one-parent household. We saw very little of our mother because she went to school in the daytime and worked at night to make a better life for us. I know first-hand the toll poverty has on a person's emotional wellbeing. I am a survivor of a system created to keep the wealthy at the top while the poor struggle to achieve a better life. My way of escaping poverty was joining the Armed Forces, the United States Army. Not everyone was fortunate to leave the toxic environment of poverty, even with college degrees. If you think impoverished communities are an eyesore, think about the people living there. I know many of them, and they didn't ask to be neglected by the highest leadership level in the United States.

Acknowledgments

I thank God for His mercy in my life. I may not have always done everything He has told me to do, but He never gave up on me. There is not enough space to give accolades to everyone in my life so, I will say it like this, you know who you are; thank you for being there for me. Thank you for sharing your knowledge and wisdom with me. Finally, I want to thank everyone for struggling and not giving up on living a decent life. Help is coming. Hold on!

About the Author

Clifton Bryant Jr retired from the U.S. Army. He continues to serve by working for the Department of Veterans Affairs, helping Veterans gain their benefits. He advocates higher learning for everyone. he has numerous degrees and educational certificates of completion. Recreational hobbies include creative writing and photography. He has a passion for helping others. Clifton is the father of twin daughters.

Contents

1. Why does America's social class system manufacture poverty?.......1

2. We need leadership that will benefit those living in poverty........23

3. How poverty affects everything around You................................32

4. How will you address the Need for Social Welfare Reform?........68

5. Does Poverty Discriminate?..86

6. Why can't the poor survive on SSI?...98

7. How about we use some of our Foreign Aid funding to help OUR poor?.................................104

8. Serving our Active Duty Servicemembers as they serve Us!.......111

9. Save our Veterans 118

10. VBA employee Woes...125

11. Everyone, especially the poor wants the truth from Politicians!...134

12. Final Thoughts..145

Chapter 1

Why does America's social class system manufacture poverty?

"The American Dream is an ideology in the United States in which freedom includes the possibility of prosperity and success to all, regardless of social class or race."

3. (Leahasilver, "Social Class in America," WordPress, 21 July 2011, https://leahasilver.wordpress.com).

This is simply not true. Everyone who sets their goals to become a physician, entrepreneur, lawyer, professional athlete, musician, software creator, fashion designer, published author, and other careers of their choosing won't achieve the American dream no matter how hard they try. Is there a reason for this misfortune and those who experience the "open window of opportunity" to others?

It's no coincidence that the poor continue to get poorer, and the wealthy become wealthier in America. Is it the lack of work ethics (for some, yes), or something or someone(s) in control of who advances and who stays behind? The recorded number of people living in poverty in the United States is 34 million, and this number will increase by 21 million due to the coronavirus pandemic.

4. (Mehrabi, Emma, "Poverty in the U.S. will reach drastic levels because of Covid-19", Children's defense fund, 21 April 2020, (https://www.childrensdefense.org/blog/poverty-in-the-u-s-will-reach-drastic-levels-because-of-covid-19/?gclid=Cj0KCQjwyZmEBhCpARIsALIzmnINxR6L03oF8QjnfDZtHV4gp5k-esu_dRG1DYOm9WmSRyLQMNZZjSsaAnmiEALw_wcB.)

Something's wrong with America having such a high percentage of poverty in a nation considered one of the wealthiest on the planet. The most prominent reason for this catastrophe on human advancement is the United States continuation to use the outdated format called the social-class system, a method of controlling the classifying people based on their income earning capabilities with a history span from 1865 to the present.

How would you feel, knowing your future is decided before you were born? Life isn't a science-fiction movie. No one should have their destiny because of the income of their parents and the geographical location of their birth. If you were born poor, chances are you will remain poor, not because of a lack of efforts to escape poverty. The impoverished are victims of a class system created to make sure this country has a working class to do the labor needed to the middle, upper and elite flourish. Unlike slavery, color, religious affiliation, or gender is not an issue. Everyone suffers. We need to end the social class system in favor of an opportunistic system that provides equality for all.

Excuses made to justify the social class System

While in the Army, we used this saying, "the maximum effective range of an excuse is zero!" Try explaining this to the wealthy as they rationalize why we have so many people living in poverty in the U.S. They make comments such as, "It is not my fault they were born poor." "Lazy people won't prosper." "They are always looking for a handout," but the one I find detestable is this, "They must like living on government assistance; otherwise, they would've done something to change their life!" How can one change their situation when someone else is playing puppeteer with your livelihood? The wealthy did not get that memo. The poor are the victims of a social class system, but how many social class systems exist and why?

The Classification of People in Society

Americans love to categorize everything. If you go to the grocery and department stores, you will find everything sorted by items, from clothes to electronics. Movies are grouped by ratings from G for general audience, PG-13 for Parental Guidance, R or restricted, to NC-17 No one under 17. It should be no surprise that we organize people into social class systems; based on economics, their monthly or annual earnings, race, religious or non-religious affiliation, you get the picture. What are the social class systems of America?

Social Class System Defined

There are many definitions regarding social class used in the United States, including Americans, by two elements: income and location. Before understanding the poverty level, you must comprehend all three social-economic class system levels and how we still have 34 million living in the lower-class social order.

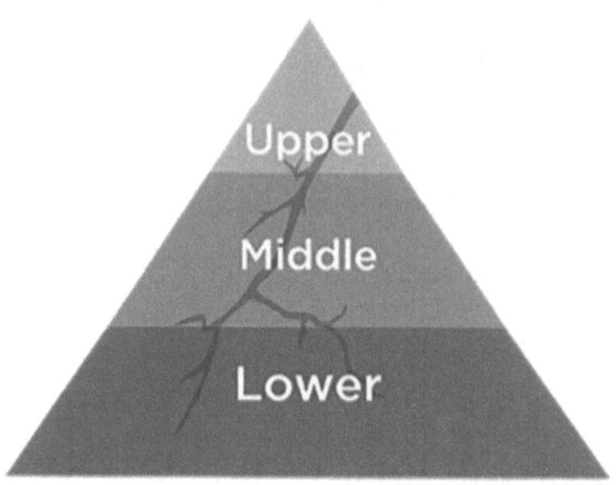

The only way the lower-class social order will change for the better is the opening of the doors that prevent them from climbing the ladder of success. There are five social class orders. The last two are working class and underclass, but they fall under the lower-class social order. The best definition of social classification is mentioned

5. (8.3 Social Class in the United States", Sociology, University of Minnesota, (https://open.lib.umn.edu/sociology/chapter/8-3-social-class-in-the-united-states/).

The upper class in the United States consists of about 4% of all households and possesses much wealth, power, and influence. Steven Martin – Highland Park Mansion – CC BY-NC-ND 2.0.

The Upper Class

Depending on how it is defined, the upper class consists of about 4% of the U.S. population and includes households with annual incomes (2009 data) of more than $200,000 (DeNavas-Walt, Proctor, & Smith, 2010). Some scholars would raise the ante further by limiting the upper class to households with incomes of at least $500,000 or so, which in turn reduces this class to about 1% of the population, with an average wealth (income, stocks and bonds, and real estate) of several million dollars. However, the upper class has much wealth, power, and influence (Kerbo, 2009).

Members of the *upper-upper* class have "old" money that has been in their families for generations; some boast of their ancestors coming over on the ship called the *Mayflower*. They belong to exclusive clubs and live in exclusive neighborhoods; have their names in the *Social Register*; send their children to expensive private schools; serve on the boards of museums, corporations, and major charities; and exert much influence on the political process and other areas of life from behind the scenes.

Members of the *lower-upper* class have "new" money acquired through hard work, lucky investments, and/or athletic prowess. In many ways, their lives are similar to those of their old-money counterparts, but they do not enjoy the prestige that old money brings. Bill Gates, the founder of Microsoft and the richest person in the United States in 2009, would be considered a lower-upper class member because his money is too "new." Because he does not have a long-standing pedigree, upper-upper class members might even be tempted to disparage his immense wealth, at least in private.

The upper-middle class in the United States consists of about 4.4% of all households, with incomes ranging from $150,000 to $199,000. Alyson Hurt – Back Porch – CC BY-NC 2.0.

The Middle Class

Many of us like to think of ourselves in the middle class—many of us are. The middle class includes 46% of all households whose annual incomes range from $50,000 to $199,999. As this overly broad range suggests, the middle class includes people with many different levels of education and income and many different types of jobs. It is thus helpful to distinguish the *upper-middle* class from the *lower-middle* class on the upper and lower ends of this income bracket, respectively.

The upper-middle class has household incomes from about $150,000 to $199,000, amounting to about 4.4% of all households. People in the upper-middle-class typically have college and, very often, graduate or professional degrees; live in the suburbs or in fairly expensive urban areas; and are bankers, lawyers, engineers, corporate managers, and financial advisers, among other occupations.

The lower-middle class has household incomes from about $50,000 to $75,000-$150,000, amounting to about 18% of all families. People in this income bracket typically work in white-collar jobs as nurses, teachers, and the like. Many have college degrees, usually from the less prestigious colleges, but many also have two-year degrees or only a high school degree. They live somewhat comfortable lives but can hardly afford to go on expensive vacations or buy expensive cars and can send their children to expensive colleges only if they receive significant financial aid.

The lower class or poor in the United States -Southside Chicago, Illinois

Lower-Class

Although "lower class" is a common term, many observers prefer a less negative-sounding term like "the poor," which is the term used here. The poor have household incomes under $25,000 and constitute about 25% of all U.S. households. Many poor lack high school degrees and are unemployed or employed only part-time in semiskilled or unskilled jobs.

They work as janitors, house cleaners, migrant laborers, and shoe shiners when they do work. They tend to rent apartments rather than own homes, lack medical insurance, and have inadequate diets.

The U.S. Poverty Statistics Report in September 2019

The United States Census Bureau released its U.S. Poverty Statistics Report in September 2019. The report confirms our government is aware of this situation. If 34 million people are living in poverty, the question of the decade is this: "What are they doing with this data?"

6. "U.S. Poverty Statistics," Federal Safety Net, (http://federalsafetynet.com/us-poverty-statistics.html/).

There is enough data from the Census Bureau to go before Congress and demand some action to reduce the number of people living in poverty in America. This is a national embarrassment! Look at the chart below and ask yourself if you are in one of these categories?

Adults not working	30%
Adults with a disability	26%
Adults without a high school diploma	26%
Single moms	25%
Black Americans	21%
Foreign-born noncitizens	18%
Hispanic Americans	18%
All children	16%
Single dads	13%
Seniors	10%
Married couples	5%
Adults with college degree or higher	4%
Full-time working adults	2%

Can we Finish the War on Poverty Started in 1964?

President Lyndon B. Johnson declared war on poverty during his State of the Union address on 8 January 1964. Since that time, America has not had another POTUS who has taken the fight to poverty on the level President Johnson initiated to create Americans' social welfare system. Here we are, 56 years later, still fighting the war on poverty, only cracking the glass ceiling when it should have been resolved.

We are on the losing end of the war on poverty. According to the Income and Poverty in the United States: 2020 report created by the United States Census (census.org), we still have 34 million people living in poverty in the United States. The time is now for the U.S. to pull out the heavy artillery and drop some state-of-the-art bombs on this enemy called the war on poverty! We need a president that is willing to finish the fight President Lyndon B. Johnson started!

Why Is It So Difficult to End the War on Poverty?

Why are our political leaders so hesitant in ending poverty in the United States? Maybe because poverty is a multi-trillion-dollar business. Too many people profit from the poor. Using a train as an example, you have the poor (working class) as the engine running the country, while the middle-class (conductors) make sure the working class stays busy and the upper-class (passengers), well, they go along for the ride at everyone's expense. The rich stay wealthy while the poor continue to labor and dream.

How Does One Become Impoverished?

Whether some start their life with high hopes of a brighter future, or some fall on hard times, the path to impoverishment is different. Some will overcome the gravitational pull of poverty, and some will not (ok, a lot won't escape). In either case, there is a method to this madness that leads to impoverishment. These are just a few:

Impoverished Category #1
Born into Poverty

Many people are born poor. According to their social status system, they are the parent(s) and children identified as living in poverty. They are the victims of forward progression, the advancement of the economy with the stabilization of one's income at the same time. What type of hope motivates you to succeed when your only employment is working at Target, Walmart, Kroger, McDonald's, Burger King, Pizza Hut, the local grocery, and pharmacy store. Sure, there is room for advancement in these establishments, but what happens when you want to be something other than the previously mentioned professions? What if you have no desire to work at the factory or the coal mines for the rest of your days?

We often mimic our surroundings. If you are living in poverty, you eventually believe this is all life has to offer. If your parent(s) worked a job with no career growth, we think it's acceptable for us. Only those not willing to settle and become poverty-stricken find a way to overcome the obstacles that held their parents back and manage to escape the stranglehold of poverty, but these are a few.

Growing up in a community that has the appearance of a post-apocalyptic movie does not provide hope for a new beginning. It is depressing; it drains you of your life energy, resulting in your disparity. It is easy giving up when you cannot see a future. Here is my example. I grew up on the Southside of Chicago until I left after joining the U.S. Army at 17. One memory that resonates with me is this: I revisited the neighborhood where I grew up and discovered a vacant lot where I once was raised.

The more the world changes, the more things remain the same

What signs of economic growth exist in the inner cities? Churches are within three buildings of each other, billboards advertising alcohol and cigarettes, and the development of Walmart's, Target's, and Sam Clubs. What isn't happening? Developers are not beautifying the Southside of inner cities. I have been gone for 32 years, and nothing on the Southside of Chicago looks new. How can someone dream of advancing when all they see is the reality of their nightmare?

Impoverished Category #2
Falling on Hard Times

If this were a movie, I would say, "Take one. Action!" You have everything; you drive the most exotic cars, take weekend getaways on your yacht, your jet is on standby to take you across America just for lunch. You throw the best parties in your mansion. You are a success story! Then, the stock market crashes, and your boss is arrested for embezzlement (sorry, stealing).

"Action!" Your life now resembles the opening scene from *Rocky V*. You lost everything. Your job, your income, the home, the cars, the yacht, and the private jet! Everything you worked for is gone, just like that! Regardless of how it happened, you are broke, and like in the movie, you are moving back into the neighborhood you escaped vowing never to return. Anyone can fall on hard times. How do you recover from losing everything you worked so hard to achieve?

Some people find a way to return to their former glorious social class status, while others never recover. The cost of surviving means you swallow your pride, apply for social welfare subsidy assistance, and seek a job with ancillary benefits and less pay. Living in the impoverished community is often hindered by these obstacles:

1. Looking for affordable, safe, and updated housing
2. Trying to stretch your EBT card so you can eat for the entire month

3. Change in the type of food you consume because of your decreased income (This usually means more fast food and less nutritious food because it is expensive.)
4. Skipping meals, so your family has more to eat
5. Working one to three jobs to survive
6. How to make it paycheck to paycheck?
7. Raising your children in an atmosphere that has zero inspirations of hope for a better tomorrow
8. Living in a community where people do not see the "promises" of voting
9. Knowing someone or turning to illegal activities to put food on your table
10. Turning to alcohol and recreational drugs to cope with your state of depression.

Impoverished Category #3
Unnatural Selection (the Birth of the Term "Impoverishment")

Darwin's theory of evolution is the process of *natural selection* by which *nature* selects the fittest, best-adapted organisms to reproduce, multiply, and survive. What man did was change the natural selection to selected nature, choose who will advance, and remain in poverty.

During his motivational speech, "I have a dream," at the Civil Rights March in Washington, 28 August 1963, the late Dr. Martin

Luther King Jr. echoed these immortal words: "We hold these truths to be self-evident: that all men are *created* equal."

Some believe in Darwin's Theory of Evolution, while others believe in the God-creation theory. I want to point this out: If Darwin were correct, why would man interfere with the creation by developing a social class system?

We know everyone can be whatever they want to be in America, right? Just because you were born in poverty doesn't mean you have to remain there. This is America, right? The land of the free and the home of the brave! You can be anything you want, right? Sadly, this isn't true anymore. The reason is simple: *unnatural development has replaced the creation selection!*

Living in poverty brings clarity to one thing; in the beginning, man created it to steal your ambition, ideas, hope, and self-esteem. Like quicksand, it will pull you under, and without a lifeline, you will suffocate. That is the actual effect of poverty.

Maybe that is one of the reasons you hear people that have made it out say, "I'm never coming back, not even to visit!" The fear of returning is so overwhelming; it is claustrophobic.

Why would the government allow poverty to occur?

The government created the social systems for a reason; somebody must labor (lower class), someone must manage the employers (middle class), and someone must reap the benefits of all that hard-earned labor (upper class).

For years we have been told that people who do not try hard enough do not want to succeed. That simply is not true. Picture this: What happens when an unmovable object (your will and all your talent, dreams, and aspirations) meets an irresistible force (the systems in place to block forward progress.) Something is going to give. In life, without assistance, people give up. Not because they are weak or a loser, they lost hope and succumbed to no longer battling the government; the feeling of hopelessness makes you focus on your reality and not your dreams. This mindset must change.

"Some of the groups on this list are more likely to grow up in difficult homes, poor neighborhoods, and inadequate school systems. They face discrimination and limited work or advancement opportunities and the effects of generational poverty, all of which make it more likely they will live in poverty."

7. (Sauter, Michael, "The Face of Poverty," 24/7 Wallst, 1 November 2020, (https://247wallst.com/special-report/2018/09/28/faces-of-poverty/). These are the faces of poverty

1. Single recent mothers

> Poverty rate: 44.3%

> Total in poverty: 592,588

> Unmarried recent mothers as a percentage of U.S. population: 0.4%

> Unmarried recent mothers as a percentage of poor population: 1.4%

2. The unemployed

> Poverty rate: 30.4%

> Total in poverty: 2.6 million

> Unemployed as a percentage of U.S. population: 2.7%

> Unemployed as a percentage of poor population: 6.1%

3. Americans with a disability

> Poverty rate: 25.7%

> Total in poverty: 9.6 million

> Disabled as a percentage of U.S. population: 11.8%

> Disabled as a percentage of poor population: 22.6%

4. American Indian and Alaska Natives

> Poverty rate: 25.4%

> Total in poverty: 670,571

> American Indian and Alaska Natives as a percentage of U.S. population: 0.8%

> American Indian and Alaska Natives as a percentage of poor population: 1.6%

5. Adults with less than a high school diploma

> Poverty rate: 24.7%

> Total in poverty: 6.3 million

> Adults without a high school diploma as a percentage of U.S. population: 8.1%

> Adults without a high school diploma as a percentage of poor population: 14.9%

6. Black and African Americans

> Poverty rate: 23.0%

> Total in poverty: 9.1 million

> African Americans as a percentage of U.S. population: 12.5%

> African Americans as a percentage of poor population: 21.4%

7. Non-citizen immigrants

> Poverty rate: 20.4%

> Total in poverty: 4.5 million

> Non-citizens as a percentage of U.S. population: 7.0%

> Non-citizens as percentage of poor population: 10.6%

8. Children under five

> Poverty rate: 20.2%

> Total in poverty: 3.9 million

> Children under five as a percentage of U.S. population: 6.1%

> Children under five as a percentage of poor population: 9.2%

9. Hispanics and Latinos

> Poverty rate: 19.4%

> Total in poverty: 11.2 million

> Hispanics and Latinos as a percentage of U.S. population: 18.2%

> Hispanics and Latinos as a percentage of poor population: 26.2%

10. Women

> Poverty rate: 14.5%

> Total in poverty: 23.6 million

> Women as percentage of U.S. population: 51.0%

> Women as percentage of poor population: 55.4%

11. Service workers

> Poverty rate: 10.7%

> Total in poverty: 26.2 million

> Service workers as a percentage of U.S. population: 8.2%

> Service workers as a percentage of poor population: 6.6%

Our national tragedy isn't people living in poverty but the system that created poverty. The statistics previously mentioned adds up to 34 million people living in poverty. We can no longer ignore this issue.

What to do when you are tired of living in poverty?

Everyone wants to live the "American dream," from immigrants entering the U.S. in 1492 to those brought as slave labor as early as the 1500s. No one asked to be born and raised into poverty. Overcoming poverty will be no small task; you must prepare yourself for the battle to end poverty in your life!

Sacrifices

Gaining a higher education is the first step in the right direction. It is also a stumbling block because everyone can't afford to attend the next-level educational requirements. For this reason, people are passed over for job promotions as they watch a young college student with no experience become their "boss." A sacrifice is required on your part to find the energy and funding to excel in academia. If you qualify for a car loan, you can be eligible for a student loan or a personal loan for a start-up business—no more excuses.

Overcoming poverty relies on changing the way you think. Invest in your future. Use your resources wisely by spending more on educational, small business equipment, anything with entertainment as a last. I'm not saying you don't need to unwind. All fun and no progress make escaping poverty a complex task.

Finally, have the courage to see your vision through. Just because you are surrounded by those who abandoned their dreams doesn't mean you need to follow.

Beat the system by thinking more on the positive than negative. Learn to escape by doing different things, similar to what your future career should be. Associate yourself with those you aspire to become. Yes, you will love friends, you will gain a happier disposition as you get closer to your dream to become someone successful.

Do your Homework

The gaining of knowledge and wisdom is the next step. There are over 80+social welfare programs created by the government. Use the internet to research government-funded programs that provide a way out of poverty.

8. (Jeffrey, Terence P., "List of 80+ Federal Welfare Program", Single Mother Guide, Updated 16 February 2020, (https://singlemotherguide.com/federal-welfare-programs).

Think outside the Box!

The rules of social welfare programs are simple, obey the rules, and you will receive a check that allows you to make it to the next payday. The problem is you aren't surviving; you're barely floating in the water. Think about this, who depends upon you remaining in the lower-class system the most? The upper-class and the elitist. We must have a labor source, or America would sink; it's that simple. The less they pay you equates to the more they keep for themselves. You work hard, and they vacation harder; go figure.

Now, look what happens to those who think outside the box. The entrepreneurs, the professional athletes, musicians, etc., figured it out. All successful people have one thing in common; they learned to walk away from the "expectations of their environment" and do their best with their talent.

Looking at voting from a different View

For decades we have given away our right to vote by not voting at all. Why continue to allow politicians to remain in power and cater to special interest groups and not to ourselves? It will help if you become an active voter in every election. Judges Sheriff, Alderperson, Congressperson, vote!

For every election you sit out, no matter the excuse, you consent to allow elected officials to live "high on the hog," which is why you continue to beg for scraps. Politicians take care of themselves. Look at the rights granted because you choose not to vote:

1. Send their children to private schools.
2. Shop in the best stores.
3. Go on more vacations in one year than you in five!
4. Accumulate a healthy savings account for a rainy day and retirement.

Make every election count! Congress is made up of 435 House and 100 Senate seats. We must vote for politicians willing to take on the war of poverty.

1. The House seats every two years.
2. Senate seats every six years.

Don't throw away your power to change your circumstances. America will become the new third world of poverty if our politicians continue ignoring the issues important to you!

Chapter 2

We need leadership that will benefit those living in poverty

When the Republicans had the White House and Congress, they didn't forget about taking care of the poor; they didn't do it! Leadership doesn't discriminate, but we saw first-hand how the wealthy and special interest groups received "elite" treatment away from the prying eyes of the public. For four years, they neglected the issues crippling the poor. We can only pray with a new balance of power in Congress and the White House; we will have a form of leadership that doesn't neglect those in need, the poor. Can we reverse the image of scarred America from the Trump era?

America needs to Heal Thyself

America can never be a great nation until we provide the poor with the resources necessary to prosper above the poverty level. I understand, everyone living in poverty won't make the journey because of their mental conditioning, but give those who have that fighting spirit the opportunity to advance. The Biden administration possesses the new type of leadership America needs; the willingness to care for the underdog.

The attributes of a Leader

Regardless of political affiliations, a leader with the right attributes can fix anything broken in America. And fo the last four years, this type of leadership was absent as poverty numbers continued to rise as well as the neglect in "news coverage." George Friedman's, "How Important Is the US President-or Any Leader?" | lists examples of what to look for in American Leadership.

9. Geopolitical Futures, 10 November 2016, (https://geopoliticalfutures.com/how-important-is-the-us-president-or-any-leader/).

What are the key points worth embracing as a Leader

"A *leader* becomes an icon of all the hopes of a nation. "*Leaders* aren't iconic; they are human beings. The idea that they will rebuild society in a manner that is more just to one group vastly overstates their power."

"In thinking about the presidency – or political leaders anywhere – it is important to distinguish between ambitions and constraints. Giving presidents the benefit of the doubt that they meant what they said during a campaign, it must be remembered that *the president's powers by design are limited.*"

Good leaders tackle poverty, racism, gun violence, injustice within the legal system, etc., while they have the power to make a change and not wait until the next election to discuss. According to data from worldbank.org, 328.24 million people are living in the United States as of 2019. Thirty-four million live in impoverished conditions.

Timeless Presidential Quotes

The complexity of leadership requires those who seek after and gain leadership positions not to rely on their individual standards of achievement that lead their positions of power, but their willingness to adopt other measures of leadership from their predecessors with the people in mind. They must learn from past leaders to be better leaders of today and in the future. Read what past Presidents have to say

10. (Roody, David Rooy, "15 Timeless Presidential Quotes on Leadership for Presidents Day" Inc., 19 February 2018, https://www.inc.com/david-van-rooy/15-timeless-presidential-quotes-for-presidents-day.html.)

George Washington: "99% of failures come from people who make excuses."

John Adams: "If your actions inspire others to dream more, learn more, do more, and become more, you are a leader."

Thomas Jefferson: "Whenever you do a thing, act as if all the world were watching."

John Quincy Adams: "If your actions inspire others to dream more, learn more, do more, and become more, you are a leader."

Andrew Jackson: "Any man worth his salt will stick up for what he believes right, but it takes a slightly better man to acknowledge instantly and without reservation that he is in error."

Martin Van Buren: "It is easier to do a job right than to explain why you didn't."

Theodore Roosevelt: "It is hard to fail, but it is worse never to have tried to succeed."

Harry S. Truman: "It's amazing what you can accomplish if you do not care who gets the credit."

Dwight D. Eisenhower: "By leadership, we mean the art of getting someone else to do something that you want to be done because he wants to do it, not because your position of power can compel him to do it."

John F. Kennedy: "Efforts and courage are not enough without purpose and direction."

Gerald R. Ford: "Never be satisfied with less than your very best effort. If you strive for the top and miss, you'll still 'beat the pack.'"

William J. Clinton: "If you live long enough, you'll make mistakes."

Barack Obama: "Change will not come if we wait for some other person, or if we wait for some other time."

What Is the Right Form of Ethics and Compliance for Leaders to Follow?

Forbes.com provided the answers with urgency and an appealing manner to all leaders in two words, "LISTEN UP!" something leaders don't do today. Ask their subordinates, and they will say the same thing.

"Ethics refers to well-founded standards of right and wrong that prescribe what humans ought to do, usually in terms of rights, obligations, benefits to society, fairness, or specific virtues. Ethics, for example, refers to those standards that impose the reasonable obligations to refrain from rape, stealing, murder, assault, slander, and fraud."

11. Weinstein, Bruce, "What's the Difference Between Compliance and Ethics?", Forbes, 9 May 2019, (https://www.forbes.com/sites/bruceweinstein/2019/05/09/whats-the-difference-between-compliance-and-ethics/#38c540ef7524.)

How Do We Define Ethics?

"Ethics is harder to define than compliance because it involves abiding by one's personal code of conduct. Everyone has their own ethics. There isn't a universal rule, if you will, for ethics. But ethics, in essence, is about doing the right thing."

—Gerry Zack, SCCE and HCCA

"*Ethics* is what we teach to help others make good choices, both inside and outside the bounds of the official rules."

—Kortney Nordrum, Deluxe

"*Ethics* is behaving in a manner that aligns with values such as respect, trust, integrity."

—Terri Civitello, Otis Elevator

"Rules matter, but culture and ethics matter more. Companies may have written, available policies, processes, and training to all employees under their payrolls. However, if the company has a weak culture, none of its controls, policies, or procedures will matter. Instead, in companies with inferior cultures, employees tend to act in ways that harm the company's reputation, increase the risk of compliance failures and act in ways that can lead to illegal and/or fraudulent conduct."

—Tate, Intel

How Do We Define Compliance?

"Compliance is a framework for ensuring an organization and its people comply with laws and regulations that apply to it and minimizing the risk of noncompliance," notes Gerry Zack, CEO of both the Society for Corporate Compliance and Ethics (SCCE) and the Health Care Compliance Association (HCAA). "One of the many facets of a compliance program is ethics."

"*Compliance* is abiding by all the rules, all the time," maintains Terri Civitello, Associate Director, Ethics and Compliance for Otis Elevator.

Presidential Values

We are the only nation with a Pledge of Allegiance that states, "One nation under God," which means we have higher standards than the rest. Only the POTUS can show the entire world how a POTUS should act towards our own and others. We have the right to demand our President display integrity that upholds the American spirit. Winslow Myers does an excellent job detailing the values of a sitting president.

12. Myers, Winslow, "Regardless of party, what we need in a president," Times Herald, 12 July 2018, https://www.thetimesherald.com/story/opinion/columnists/2018/07/12/regardless-party-need-president/36809789/).

- A president needs to be a national model for truth-telling, encouraging and validating the scientific method, and making policy based upon experimentally validated data.
- A president needs to be a national model for truth-telling, encouraging and validating the scientific method, and making policy based upon experimentally validated data.
- A president needs a secure, private, inner-directed self-sense that transcends their image in the media, a self-sense that includes a reliable, ethical compass.
- A president needs to improve, not exacerbate, conservative–progressive polarization, and consistently emphasize what all of us have in common as Americans, like equality of opportunity and equality under the law.

- A president needs to understand racism, which is one of America's original sins so that they can actively encourage the change in behavior where everyone is respected and made to feel equal.
- Anyone who wins the presidency will inevitably possess a healthy ego, but presidents must sublimate their self-confidence into a little awareness of their position as servant leaders.
- A president needs excellent listening skills. Most of America's difficulties, domestic or international, have in common some failure to listen.
- A president needs to separate from business interests clearly and absolutely while in office.
- A president needs an authentic life experience that has tested them.
- A president needs a sense of humor, especially about themselves.
- A president needs to be a scholar of the lessons of the history of POTUS and how they fixed and not tore down American values.
- A president needs to be strong enough to push back against establishment groupthink from whatever political direction, such as the momentum of American techno-colonialism and militarism.
- Irrespective of the party, a president needs to understand the great global challenge of environmental stress, and the imperative for greater international cooperation to help the

planet through to a place where humans have learned to sustain the commons that is the life support system for all.

- A president must understand that many of our contemporary challenges are transnational and that the delicate structures of international law must be strengthened. This will unquestionably benefit America's security in the long term.
- A president needs discernment. As my father used to say, quoting Leo Rosten: "First-rate people hire first-rate people. Second-rate people hire fourth-rate people."

Of course, every trait that makes a good president also makes a good citizen. If we want a better president, we must first endorse better values within ourselves! Only then will we choose a leader who reflects our image to the entire world with pride and not shame! Only the POTUS can determine how history will shape your America's legacy. Do you want to be known as a great role model or a global embarrassment to Americans?

Chapter 3

How poverty affects everything around You

"Being a product of solely your environment conjures up a disturbing image of humans lying on an assembly line being sent to predestined locations. Life is not like that. Nonetheless, that's not to say the environment cannot drastically manipulate the "product."

13. 1. FlowerofScotland, Glasgow, Other, "You Are A Product Of Your Environment" teenink.com, 11/8/2015, https://www.teenink.com/opinion/social_issues_civics/article/838629/You-Are-A-Product-Of-Your-Environment. Assessed on 10/16/2021.

There's nothing more insulting than someone making this statement about you because you grew up on the poverty side of the tracks. The environment worsens poverty and this is a fact.

If poverty is an eyesore, imagine what life is for those who live It?

New Jersey Detroit

Chicago Mississippi

"Hideous, right? That's because, in the U.S., we hide our slums with advertisements to visit the "richest part" of our major cities. You won't find those living in poverty unless you are on the Southside of cities. We keep them hidden and redirect your attention to the cement walls, redirected thoroughfares, and sprawling suburbs. They're usually tucked around the freeways in great neighborhoods with one way in and one way out. I have witnessed this myself on the west coast, just outside of Hella and Griffith Park, while trying to avoid the freeway during rush hour. The houses/domiciles were little squares on patches of dirt, broken fences, and press-board shanties in between. Growing up in a small town, this is the worst that I had seen."

14. Hedges, Chris, "Recalled to Life," Harig, Amanda, Quora, 25 February 2015, (https://www.quora.com/What-is-the-biggest-slum-in-the-U-S-and-why).

"This is something they do not teach in school. The 19th-Century New York City Neighborhood That Invented Tap Dance, Stole Elections, and Became the World's Most Notorious Slum. By 1813 it had been filled in, and by 1825 something entirely new stood on the site America's first real slum, the Five Points."

15. (Baker, Kevin, "The First Slum in America," The New York Times, 30 September 2001, https://www.nytimes.com/2001/09/30/books/the-first-slum-in-america.html).

Remember this idiom, "See no evil, Hear no evil, Speak no evil," because this is how our middle and upper class treats the poor.

The press will not cover it, the housing developers will not discuss it, and lawmakers will not mention it. The lower-class communities of America are slowly taking on the third-world countries' image; we send billions of dollars to provide relief to the poor in other countries, but what about the poor in our own backyard? Let's address these issues.

Unsafe Environments

Imagine growing up as a child in the 80's entertaining yourself in poverty-stricken communities. Armed with only your imagination and creativity to keep yourself from being bored out of your mind. you played games like "jumping off porches onto discarded bed mattresses, playing hide-and-go-seek in abandoned and /or fire-damaged buildings and homes. We increased the stakes by playing games that required locking ourselves into disregarded trucks and refrigerators just to see how long we could hold our breath and even greater risky games like "jumping the train", that's when you jumped onto a moving train and rode it for a few blocks. That was our fun.

Playing in the inner city didn't come without risks, sometimes our fun put us in harm's way such as injuring yourselves by getting suck by a hypodermic needles, cutting yourself on broken glass, stepping on rusty nails, scratching your flesh on splintered wood, twisting your ankle in a hole, or worse, getting raped, robbed, or murdered.

Today is no different. When you look at all the issues inner city children encounter when playing outdoors, it's no wonder there is a multi-billion-dollar game industry; there is no safe place for children to play outdoors. What other actions are affected by poverty daily.

Dangers you can't See!

There are other dangers of living in poverty-stricken communities. The hazards that you cannot see but are very real and very deadly. Their bites are just as bad as their names. I am referring to bacterial diseases caused by, for example, Streptococcus pyogenes, commonly known as flesh-eating bacteria. This type of infection enters the body by way of bacteria through a cut or other open wound in the skin. Methicillin-resistant Staphylococcus aureus (MRSA), other bacteria capable of causing severe health issues, is spread through physical contact and must breach the skin through a cut to create the infection. Hepatitis C is a liver disease caused by contact such as hugging, kissing, sharing cups, plates, eating, or cooking utensils.

And then there's *Lockjaw* or ***Tetanus,*** a disease that enters the body through deep cuts or wounds, and these spores grow into bacteria that produce a toxin known as tetanospasmin, which affects the nervous system. One can contract Tetanus from puncture wounds from splinters, nails, body piercings, or illicit drug injections, gunshots, fractures and burns, animal or insect bites, ulcers in the foot, even dental infections.

Drug Epidemic: Deal with it Now or Pay for it Later!

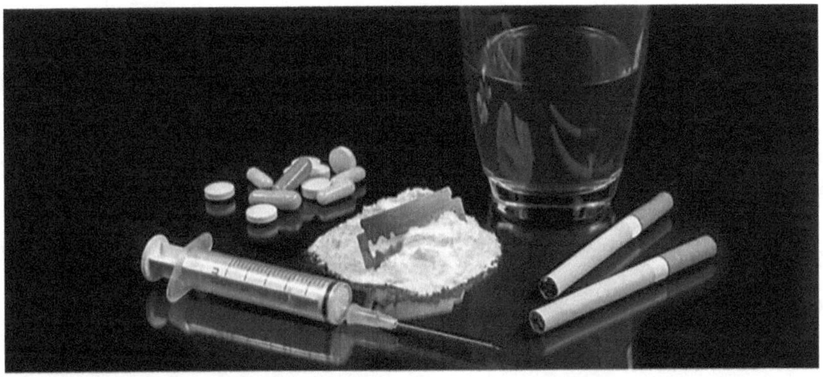

The United States have a major drug problem. It's everywhere; the inner cities, suburbia, and the upper/ elite social status areas of our country. For those living in poverty, several studies have concluded people with lower income or those who live in environments that are not conducive to economic growth, are more at risk of falling victims to drug abuse.

Federal and local governments are doing everything they can to reduce overdose deaths in the country, but only after Former President Trump declared war on illegal drugs and opioid abuse, echoing his battle cry "national pandemic" in 2020, after 71,000 people died due to drug overdoses. Only then, did it make national headlines. It was compared to the AIDS epidemic of the 1980s and '90s.

The cries of "lock them up" only apply to people of color. Now we hear and see television commercials encouraging treatment at rehabilitation centers as the first choice of corrective action, but not for those born in the inner city and live in the poverty-stricken communities.

"One of the most devastating problems when considering poverty and drug addiction is the lack of access to rehabilitation and recovery. If there are no financial resources, there is no access to a rehab center, which can put a person at risk of dying from an overdose or spiraling out of control and becoming lost in their addiction forever.

The rise in criminal Activities

Have you ever wondered why the poor would rob the poor working and underclass poor people? The reason will shock some, but not everyone. Unlock Hollywood movies, people don't steal for pleasure; they steal for a reason: Survival. they want to pay their bills, live in houses, drive cars and dress nice. I don't agree with their criminal activities. If you observe the options provided to those growing up in poverty, you can see their point of view. Here are a few of them:

- The only abundance of jobs include the fast-food and storage facility industries.
- Lack of development to beautify the poor communities, which could bring in jobs.

- Lack of recourses to give the children of poverty an alternative lifestyle.
- Lack of resources for adults to attend a higher education level makes them competitive with the growing job market.

People want to live with dignity and not constantly be reminded they failed to get their families out of the poverty-stricken communities. There is no excuse for criminal behavior, but it's hard for children and adults growing up in poverty not to be envious of those engaged in illegal activities. To change the criminal, we need to change the job system to one that doesn't hold your past against you and restores your dignity or grants dignity at the same time. Only then will you get criminals off the street. ok, not all of them but a significant number will change.

The migration of gun violence from the poverty-stricken Communities

Senseless gun violence has plagued poverty-stricken communities from the time I was a toddler well into my senior adulthood. I am thankful to God that I am 54 years old, and no one is saying, "he was a good person." There is both a story and a message in what I am about to tell. Until we eliminate gun violence from the poverty-stricken communities, it will continue migrate to the middle-class and upper-class neighborhoods.

When America claims it doesn't see a thing wrong with Gun Violence until it hits home

America as a whole, doesn't see a thing wrong with Gun Violence until it hits their home. This is a true statement. When gun violence is confined to the poverty-level communities, made up of 19.1% Hispanics, 18% Whites to include White Hispanics, and 28.9% of African Americans to include Black Hispanics, America turned a blind eye. There was no reason for the alarm to be sounded.

Gun violence is used to promote someone's sick agenda; drive-by shootings, botched robberies, killing witnesses keep them from testifying, drug deals going wrong, fatal relationship disputes, or simply revenge. all this happens in the lowest communities where violence is the norm but look what happened when gun violence began the "great migration" to the middle- and upper-class communities.

Gun violence is used to promote someone's sick agenda; drive-by shootings, botched robberies, killing witnesses keep them from testifying, drug deals going wrong, fatal relationship disputes, or simply revenge. Keep in mind that crimes due to gun violence eventually migrate to middle-upper class communities. America turned that infamous bind eye until mass shootings claimed the middle and upper-class Americans' lives.

18. (https://en.wikipedia.org/wiki/List_of_mass_shootings_in_the_United_States)

List of mass shootings in the United States by number of deaths

March 31, 2021: Apartment Building in the Congress Heights area of Washington, DC- 2

March 28, 2021: Cleveland nightclub, Cleveland, Ohio-7

March 28, 2021: Essex, Maryland- 5

March 26, 2021: Virginia Beach, Virginia- 4

March 26, 2021: Memphis, Tennessee- 4

March 23, 2021: Aliceville, Alabama- 2

March 23, 2021: Boulder, Colorado- 11

March 16, 2021: Atlanta- 6

April 20, 1999: Columbine High School in Littleton, Colorado- 12

April 16, 2007: Virginia Tech University in Blacksburg, Virginia-32

December 5, 2007: Omaha, Nebraska-8

March 10, 2009: Geneva County, Alabama-23

April 3, 2009: Binghamton, N.Y.-13

November 5, 2009: Fort Hood, Texas-13

August 3, 2010: Manchester, Connecticut-8

January 8, 2011: Tucson, Arizona-6

October 12, 2011: Seal Beach, California-8

April 2, 2012: Oakland, California-7

July 20, 2012, Aurora, Colorado-12

December 14, 2012: Sandy Hook Elementary School, Newtown, Connecticut-26

March 13, 2013: Herkimer, N.Y. -4

June 9, 2013: Santa Monica, California-5

September 16, 2013: Washington, D.C.-12

February 21, 2014: Alturas, California

May 23, 2014: Isla Vista, California-6

October 24, 2014: Marysville, Washington-4

May 17, 2015: Waco, Texas-9

June 17, 2015: Charleston, South Carolina-9

July 23, 2015: Lafayette, Louisiana-3

October 1, 2015: Roseburg, Oregon-10

December 2, 2015: San Bernardino, California-14

November 27, 2015: Colorado Springs, Colorado-3

February 20, 2016: Kalamazoo, Michigan-6

February 25, 2016: Hesston, Kansas-3

June 12, 2016: Orlando, Florida-49

October 1, 2017: Paradise, Nevada-61

November 5, 2017: Sutherland, Texas-28

February 14, 2018: Parkland, Florida-17

November 7, 2018: Thousand Oaks, California-13

May 18, 2018: Santa Fe, Texas-10

August 3, 2019: El Paso, Texas-23

There are more. There's no way I could finish this book if I added all the names of victims of gun violence. It took all these and more lives to be lost outside the poverty-stricken communities before "all of America" to open its eyes to gun violence. Look at the faces of the media, politicians, parents, children, law enforcement, address senseless crimes now that the poorest communities are no longer the targets of mass shootings.

N-o-w, we see parents on CNN expressing their frustration over the federal leadership for not having stricter gun laws in place. Children were placed on buses to go to Washington to give speeches against gun violence. This was amazing! The entire country poured its heart out and wanted answers. How did this happen? What can we do to make sure it would never happen again?

The answer was simple: failure to do something when it was not their issue migrated into their communities and became their problems. All children and adults' lives should have been viewed as precious, regardless of their social background. If you want to end gun violence, you must "uproot" it at the source, the poverty-stricken communities.

A step in the right Direction

"Gun violence in this country is an epidemic, and it's an international embarrassment," President Biden spoke these words at the April 8, 2021 news conference.

19. "Okeefe, Ed, and Grace Segers, "Biden announces executive actions to curb gun violence "epidemic," April 4, 2021, CBSnews.com, (https://www.cbsnews.com/news/biden-gun-control-executive-actions-violence-epidemic/)

President Biden tackles gun violence by signing executive orders, directing the Department of Justice to spend the coming weeks developing plans to address:

1. "Ghost guns," which are handmade firearms or gun kits that the buyer assembles. Ghost guns don't need to be registered or have a serial number. The Bureau of Alcohol, Tobacco, Firearms, and Explosives doesn't regulate these kits as firearms. Democrat lawmakers want ghost guns as firearms, which would require a background check.
2. Ban on assault weapons and high-capacity magazines.
3. More stringent background checks.

Despite the president reminding Americans that his executive orders do not impinge on the 2nd Amendment rights of those who own firearms, people like the NRA and Congresspeople with supped-up security and overly tall fences cried foul.

I often wonder how a 2nd Amendment supporter would react to President Biden's efforts to end gun violence if someone they knew were shot, killed, or maimed for life with a modified weapon? Firearms are sold to the lawless who found a loophole in the current gun laws and legally purchased a weapon capable of mass destruction. It happens all the time, especially at gun shows.

What is it going to take to put an end to gun violence in America; the end of gun violence in the hood, pure and simple. when the politicians no longer profit from gun sales, we'll see a change.

How many people must die before Congress officials realize that all lives matter?

The average American citizen wants to protect their homes and families against invaders, and there's nothing wrong with that. The problem is what worked in 1975 just isn't working in 2022. People have changed, the values are different, and they are either in full anger or "full-blown" survival mode. No one is safe. The laws need to change and now.

The Perils of Public Schools in Poverty Stricken Communities

What's wrong with this picture? It's the typical image of a public school closed in poor neighborhoods. Would this happen in the middle, upper, or elite social communities? Has it come to this? The disparity of taking care of one public school system in one community while watching another public school close, namely in the impoverished communities.

The government's attempt to fix a broken public designed educational system

The Elementary and Secondary Education Act (ESEA) of 1965, originally passed as part of the Lyndon B. Johnson (DEMOCRAT) administration's War on Poverty campaign. The law's initial goal, which remains today, was to improve students' educational equity from lower-*income families by providing federal funds to school districts serving poor students.* After 55 years, the law continues to neglect the important changes that affect the mind; improving the environment raising the children.

More public schools in impoverished communities are forced to shut down their creative programs as a means of saving money. "Nearly 1 in 5 public school teachers have second jobs during the school year, a new analysis of federal data shows. Half of the teachers with second jobs work in a field outside of education, while 5 percent of teachers take on a second teaching or tutoring job outside of their school districts. And 4 percent of teachers have a job that is not teaching but is still related to the teaching field."

20. Will, Madeline, "To Make Ends Meet, 1 in 5 Teachers Have Second Jobs." Edweek.org, 6/19/ 2018, www.edweek.org/leadership/to-make-ends-meet-1-in-5-teachers-have-second-jobs/2018/06. Assessed 9/25/2021.

Studies were done proving that poverty-stricken children do not receive a fair portion of government-funded educational assistance. "The U.S. Department of Education reported in 2011 that more than 40 percent of low-income schools do not get a fair share of state and local funds. At the time, former Secretary of Education Arne Duncan acknowledged that "in far too many places, policies for assigning extra support, resources, and teachers to low-income students in need perpetuated the problem rather than solving it."

21. Taylor, Kelley, "Poverty's Long-List Effects on Students' Education and Success," insightintodiversity.org, 5/30/2017, www.insightintodiversity.com/povertys-long-lasting-effects-on-students-education-and-success. Assessed on 9/25/2021.

Keep in mind that this article was written in 2017. Do you honestly believe the educational system has changed to support or continue to restrict the educational advancements of the impoverished? If you want the true answer, ask those living in poverty.

The No Child Left Behind (NCLB) Act, signed by George W. Bush, 8 January 2002. This act replaces the Elementary and Secondary Education Act of 1965 (ESEA). The NCLB law, which grew out of concern that the American education system was no longer internationally competitive, significantly increased the federal role in holding schools responsible for all students' academic progress.

Focus on ensuring that states and schools boost the performance of certain groups of students, such as English-language learners, students in special education, poor, and minority children, whose achievement, on average, trails their peers. States did not have to comply with the new requirements, but if they didn't, they risked losing federal Title I money

22. (Klein, Alyson, "No Child Left Behind: An Overview," Education Week, 10 April 2015, https://www.edweek.org/ew/section/multimedia/no-child-left-behind-overview-definition-s23. ummary.html).

T*he Every Student Succeeds Act*, signed by President Obama on 10 December 2015, created a new measure while maintaining a handful of No Child Left Behind provisions. It most notably preserves the federal testing schedule, which requires states to test students annually in grades three through eight in reading and math, and once in high school in each subject. Also, it continued the requirement that schools annually report students' achievement scores and break down that data by race, economic status, disability, and English-learner status.

"Without that language, Democratic Sen. Cory Booker of New Jersey had threatened to filibuster the bill, and Duncan said the President would not sign it."

23. (Camera, Lauren, "No Child Left Behind Has Finally Been Left Behind," usnews.com, 9 December 2015, https://www.usnews.com/news/articles/2015/12/09/congress-replaces-no-child-left-behind-shifts-power-to-states).

Is Poverty Driving Down the Cost of Education?

"In more than half of the states in the U.S., the poorest school districts do not receive funding to address their students' increased needs – just the latest data point to shine a spotlight on funding gaps that plague the country's public education system.

School districts with the highest rates of poverty receive about $1,000 less per student in state and local funding than those with the lowest rates of poverty, according to a new report released Tuesday by The

Education Trust. While the funding gaps among states vary significantly, Illinois, Missouri, New York, and Alabama rank among the worst.

In Illinois, for example, the most impoverished districts received 22 percent less in state and local funding than the lowest-poverty districts."

24. Camera, Lauren, "In Most States, Poorest School Districts Get Less Funding," U.S.News.com, 27 February 2018, (https://www.usnews.com/news/best-states/articles/2018-02-27/in-most-states-poorest-school-districts-get-less-funding).

People living in poverty are familiar with this news. They know that public schools in impoverished communities get a minuscule budget. When your school must sell its band equipment and say goodbye to its creative programs, that is hate. The only time a child of the poverty-stricken community would see a newly developed school was driving past one and not in their neighborhood. Why is the money there for new schools in prominent districts, but lacking in impoverished areas?

If what happens regularly in the poverty-stricken communities occurred in the middle- or upper-class communities, the media would be all over it. What happens in poor neighborhoods has become socially acceptable. Children of poverty encounter one of all the following obstacles:

1. Being taught from outdated textbooks, while middle- and upper-class social students continue to learn from the latest edition of books.
2. Loss of creative school programs such as like theater and art to be available for standard teaching and sports programs.
3. Waiting until the senior year to teach college preparation classes if taught at all.

What Can Schools Do to Address Poverty?

In 2015, the article "What Can Schools Do to Address Poverty" was written. It is 2020, and nothing has changed.

25. (Parrett, William and Budge, Kathleen, "What Can Schools Do to Address Poverty?" Edutopia, 10 December 2015, https://www.edutopia.org/blog/what-can-schools-do-to-address-poverty-william-parrett-kathleen-budge)

"Eliminating poverty is a both/and proposition -- reforms must occur in *both* the broader society *and* in schools -- and schools do make a considerable difference. We encourage educators, and particularly educational leaders, to both, become knowledgeable about issues related to eliminating poverty, join forces with others who advocate for social and economic reforms, and summon the courage to do the much-needed work closer to home -- in their own schools and communities."

- Provide free computers and internet access to all students at home.

- Get parents involved with their children's learning by providing transportation, on-site childcare, and time-flexibility as needed.
- Teach about injustices disproportionately affecting the poor, preparing new students to make a more equitable world.
- Develop curricula relevant and meaningful to our students' lives and draw on their experiences and surroundings.
- Fight to get our students into gifted and talented programs, give them other opportunities usually reserved for economically advantaged students.
- Challenge our colleagues when they stigmatize poor students and their parents, reminding them of our schools and classrooms' inequitable conditions.

Eight years later:
What is the status of the Flint Water Crisis?

CNN Library

Now that the Coronavirus has become the center of attention again, there is one question that I am sure is still on the minds of the people of Flint, Michigan. When will we be allowed to drink and bathe in water in our homes again? Eight years have passed and it seems no one remembers what happened. Maybe this "Timeline of the Flint Water Crisis" will refresh your memory.

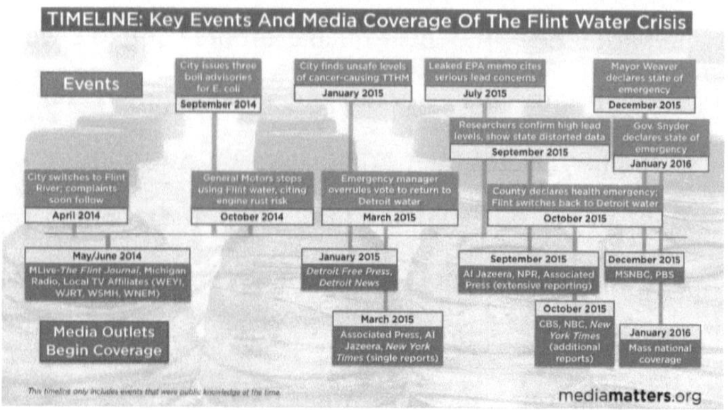

The last national media coverage was August 21, 2020. Flint residents will receive a settlement of 600 million from the Flint Water Crisis. It's a shame that it took six years for lawmakers to decide from January 2016 to the present. We can only pray the damaged health crisis from this human-made disaster can be corrected.

These are the facts about the location of the Flint, Michigan Water Crisis.

"Flint, located 70 miles north of Detroit, is a city of 99,002, where 41.6% of residents live below the poverty line, and the median household income is $24,679, according to the U.S. Census Bureau. The median household income for the rest of Michigan is $49,087. The city is 56.6% African American."

"In 2011, the state of Michigan took over Flint's finances after an audit projected a $25 million deficit. Even though Flint's water supply fund was $9 million in the red, officials used some of this money to cover shortfalls in its general fund. A receivership ended in April 2015, when the water fund was declared to be solvent, and an emergency loan eliminated the remaining deficit."

"To reduce the water fund shortfall, the city switched water sources in 2014. While a new pipeline connecting Flint with Lake Huron was under construction, the city turned to the Flint River as a water source during the two-year transition. The Flint River had been the city's primary water source decades earlier, but Flint switched to Lake Huron in 1967, purchasing its supply through the Detroit Water and Sewerage Department."

"Health effects of lead exposure in children include impaired cognition, behavioral disorders, hearing problems, and delayed puberty. In pregnant women, lead is associated with reduced fetal growth. In every one, lead consumption can impact the heart, kidneys, and nerves. Although there are medications that may reduce the amount of lead in the blood, treatments for the adverse health effects of lead have yet to be developed."

"January 14, 2016 – Governor Snyder writes President Barack Obama to request the declaration of an expedited major disaster in Flint, estimating it will cost $55 million to install lead-free pipes throughout the city."

"January 16, 2016 – The president declines to declare a disaster in Flint. Instead, he authorizes $5 million in aid, declaring a state of emergency in the city. The state of emergency allows the Federal Emergency Management Agency (FEMA) to step in."

26. "Flint Water Crisis Fast Facts," 790 KABC, 22 April 2016, (https://www.kabc.com/2016/04/22/flint-water-crisis-fast-facts/).

Takeaways about the Flint Water Crisis

Flint has a water crisis of excessive lead in their bathing and drinking water supply. 41.6% of residents live below the poverty line, and the median household income is $24,679, according to the U.S. Census Bureau. The median household income for the rest of Michigan is $49,087. The city is 56.6% African American. "Governor Snyder reached out to President Obama, requesting 55 million to handle the Flint Water Crisis. President Obama gave Flint, Michigan, the maximum He could give as a president-five million. Congress would have to vote on the rest. To date, President Obama is the only president to address Flint Water Crisis and offer federal funding."

1. Flint is 56% African American and residents living below the poverty line. Could this be the reason no real action has been taken to dissolve this water crisis? It has been seven years, just a thought.

2. Are there other cities with the same water problem? Is the government doing anything about it?

How the Covid-19 Pandemic worsened for those living in poverty

There are parts of the United States that resemble the landscapes of third-world countries. I know this to be true because I deployed to Somalia, Kosovo, and Iraq. I can say with great sadness; I felt like I was at home. I grew up in neighborhoods in the United States that looked as if it was bombed and never rebuilt. Imagine living in an environment that doesn't give you hope for a brighter future; now imagine how Covid-19 makes the poverty-stricken communities worse.

"The COVID-19 outbreak hasn't *caused* these underlying problems, but it has highlighted the deficits within the U.S.'s fragile social safety net. If low-income Americans get and spread COVID-19 at a higher rate, it's bad for everyone."

27. "Coronavirus May Disproportionately Hurt the Poor And That's Bad for Everyone," Time.com, 11 March 2020, https://time.com/5800930/how-coronavirus-will-hurt-the-poor.

Covid-19 and Economics

"Low-income jobs—line-cooks, nurse's aides, grocery store clerks, nannies—mostly can't be done remotely, and the majority of low-income jobs don't offer paid sick days. Low-income people are disproportionately more likely to be uninsured or underinsured for medical care, and for many, even stocking up the pantry can be an impossible financial hurdle. According to a 2019 Federal Reserve study, 40% of Americans could not come up with $400 to cover an emergency. Lacking resources to prepare and protect against the COVID-19, many of these individuals face a higher risk of contracting—and subsequently spreading—the virus."

Vesoulis, Abby, "Coronavirus May Disproportionately Hurt the Poor-And That's Bad for Everyone," Time.com, 11 March 2020, https://time.com/5800930/how-coronavirus-will-hurt-the-poor.

Covid-19 and congested living Arrangements

Try living in a community created to put people on top of people. Yes, I'm talking about affordable housing in the inner cities. You know I'm not talking about the suburbs. While the CDC provided guidelines for the entire nation to follow; mandatory mask-wearing when outside and in essential-labeled businesses. the problem first noticed in the inner cities was the keeping of six feet apart person.

How can you practice social distancing when you are living 5-6 deep in an apartment with three rooms? In most poverty-stricken communities, people are practically living on top of each other. Yet, they must find a way to keep the virus from spreading from one member infected to another. And your neighbors, you're practically two to four feet apart from them, good luck with that!

Covid-19 and surviving without a Job

In May 2020, Covid-19 increased the number of unemployed by 20 million. This was due to the government-mandated business closures during the first phase of the pandemic. Every business that was deemed non-essential laid off employees so they could apply for the Unemployment Insurance benefits under the CARES act, up 39 weeks of unemployment payments until 31 December 2020 if needed. People turned to food banks like never before. Cars lined up two football fields long as people were waiting to receive a lifeline of food to feed their families, and this was just the beginning.

Covid-19 and Healthcare

Poverty-stricken people are the last to trust their healthcare system. Before Obamacare, the healthcare system for poor people was terrible. Watered-down liquid meds and expired medication. Don't get me started with the long days and nights at the state ran hospitals. Now we bring the pandemic into the picture. Hospitals won't see walk-ins because they need the space for Covid-19 patients, and only the severely ill patient would be admitted. What do you do? Buy all the over-the-counter cold and flu medication you can, go to your HMO appointment clinic, and hope for the best. There is only so much room in a public hospital for the 34 million people living in poverty.

Covid-19 and Price-Gouging

With most of your expendable finances going towards over-the-counter medication to treat the Covid-19 symptoms, you have to deal with the nation-wide price gouging. A small bottle of bleach is almost $8.00, and the same is for a can of Lysol and toilet tissue. Everyone that can profit from the Pandemic is doing so except the poor. What do you do? Buy the necessities needed and cut back on groceries or sacrifice how you spend money? A problem the wealthy doesn't have, but poor people do. Make your choice.

Ok, I'm concluding this podcast by saying poverty is a national disgrace that can't be ignored. Not by the business world, the hospitals, your employers, family, friends and the healthcare industry. this is podcast is another example of the need to re-vamp our working poor and underclass sect of America before poverty turn America into the next 3rd world country.

Stay tuned for future podcasts pertaining to poverty in America as I am promoting my soon to be released book titled, "The U.S. no one is talking about." I'm your host, CB2; Clifton Bryant Jr, signing off. I'm Just Sayin…Peace.

Covid-19 and working from home

If you believe working from home is a luxury, think again. It takes a lot to prepare yourself for the workday while getting the family ready for their day. You asked to be left alone to do your job but try explaining this to your 2–3-year-old; all they understand is mommy and daddy are at home, and it's "me" time. With childcare businesses closed courtesy of the Pandemic, you became chef, organizer, schoolteacher, and employee all in the same sentence. Now add poverty to this equation. Most poor people didn't work from home; they were laid off but dealt with everything mentioned other than employment.

Covid-19 and the New Normality

The Coronavirus infected 62,762,689 people and claimed the lives of 842,141 people (as of 1/13/2021) in the U.S. People continue to lose their lives to another human-made product. Life will never return to normal because we can't bring the dead back to life. Generations of loved ones were wiped off the face of the planet. People are still suffering residuals of the Covid-19 exposure. Most people will find new jobs as part of our new normality is the acceptance that closed businesses are not reopening; from major chains to "mom and pop" stores, the damage is done. We will survive this Pandemic and live our lives under the new normality, but we will also bear the physical and mental scars of the Covid-19 Pandemic, especially the poor.

How Does Poverty Aid in the Decision for a Woman to Have an Abortion?

Since *Roe v. Wade*, a total of 62,502,904 abortions have been performed from 1973 to 2020. This number is not accurate since there is no law mandating the account of the number of abortions performed by each state to the CDC (Center for Disease Control and Prevention). Abortion is not the ideal conversational topic to discuss around the water cooler at the office, grocery shopping, spin classes, or church; however, when poverty plays a factor, it must be addressed.

There is a relationship between poverty and how abortion fits in this equation. More women living in poverty have abortions due to economic hardships than the middle and upper classes reported.

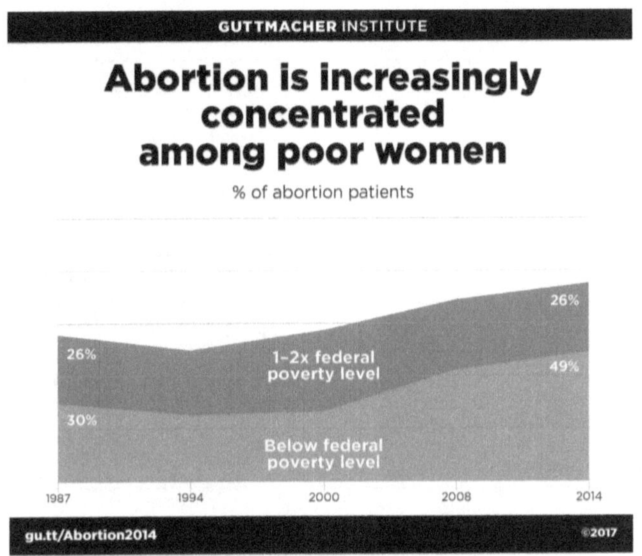

According to the chart, 26% of women have abortions at a rate of 1–2% of the federal poverty level, while 30% of women have abortions at a 1–2% rate at the national poverty level.

2020 Federal Poverty Guidelines Chart

The HHS Department issues poverty guidelines for each household size. For example, the poverty level for a household of four in 2020 is an annual income of $26,200. To get the poverty level for larger families, add $4,480 for each household's additional person. For smaller families, subtract $4,480 per person. Guidelines for Alaska and Hawaii are higher since it is more expensive to live there. The chart below calculates it for you:

Number of People in Household	48 States & DC	Alaska	Hawaii
One	$12,760	$15,950	$14,680
Two	$17,240	$21,550	$19,830
Three	$21,720	$27,150	$24,980
Four	$26,200	$32,750	$30,130
Five	$30,680	$38,350	$35,280
Six	$35,160	$43,950	$40,430
Seven	$39,640	$49,550	$45,580
Eight	$44,120	$55,150	$50,730
For nine or more, add this amount for each additional person	$4,480	$5,600	$5,15

28. (Amadeo, Kimberly| Scott, Gordon [Reviewer], "Federal Poverty Level Guidelines and Chart," The Balance, 7 February 2020, (https://www.thebalance.com/federal-poverty-level-definition-guidelines-chart-3305843#2020federal-poverty-guidelines-chart)

There are so many levels of poverty; it is no wonder people find it hard to escape. Therefore, the federal and state governments must do better subsidize the incomes and programs for impoverished women. As the woman's income rises, so does the decrease in abortions. However, if her income depletes after each paycheck, the decision to have an abortion is based on the circumstances.

- **Rape** is a violent crime, not of passion, but of taking the right of someone's decision to choose not to have sex with an individual from them.

- **Sexual assault** is an act in which a person intentionally sexually touches another person without the latter's consent or coerces or physically forces the person to engage in a sexual act against their will. How many people knew April is Sexual Assault Awareness Month?
- **Ectopic pregnancy** is when a pregnant woman's egg settles outside its usual location in the womb's inner lining. The egg cannot develop naturally, and the consequences can be severe for the woman.
- **Incest/genetic disorder** is a situation where close family members have sexual relations. This act dramatically increases the likelihood that a child born out of such a relationship will have some form of genetic deformation or retardation.
- **As a Form of Birth Control**-contraceptives available, many health clinics with a prescription while men can get them for free and purchase them at any local store.
- **Low-income women** are less likely to use contraception. They are at a higher risk for life disruptions (job loss, homelessness, falling behind on rent or mortgage payments, or separation from their partner). Several mentioned the loss of a job, which led to health insurance and access to hormonal contraceptives.
- **Realizing a poor decision is not worth reliving for the rest of your life:** The choice to have sex is that of you and your partner. Whether it be a one-night stand or continuous sexual

liaisons, think about the consequences that will last you a lifetime, something to be considered before the sexual act.

- **Having sexual relations with an unemployed person.** Really? Is it that good?
- **Your sexual partner already has children that they are not taking care of.** Why are you willing to have unprotected sex?
- **Spiritual convictions:** This is simple. A person's relationship with God aids them in their decision not to have an abortion.

The reasons men do not have a right to decide if a woman should have an abortion:

- Men do not carry babies in their bodies, and they do not go through labor!
- No laws are making a "man" provide for the mother from conception to delivery and beyond.
- Men are only thinking about themselves and not the mother and the life of the child. If they are that concerned, why won't they stay in the relationship? Any woman you deem good enough to have sex with should be good enough for you to marry or remain committed to it.
- Stop acting like an animal, "beating your chest" and saying, "I'm a proud papa," but you weren't present for the birth, through a fault of yours, while the mother hasn't seen a dime

from you and you refuse to sign the birth certificate to give the child your last name. Another act of selfishness.

How couples can provide for their baby and not go the route of abortion in the poverty-stricken Communities

- Combining incomes. Two minimum-wage-paying jobs with two forms of government subsidies income are more than enough to provide for the baby!
- Commit to being there for your child, from conception to life after high school.
- Stop being an absentee father—that era is old and dead. Let's break the cycle of what your father didn't do. Be there for your baby and the mother.

In the poverty-stricken community, no one can convince a woman not to proceed with an abortion. There is a consistent track record of the father never being around to help provide emotional and financial support from conception to delivery. Eighty-eight percent of women, particularly single women, have an abortion because they live below the poverty line. Only when the man commits to taking care of the woman he impregnated, and the child will we see a reduction in abortions in the poverty-stricken communities.

Chapter 4

How will you address the Need for Social Welfare Reform?

What is the History of the Social Welfare System?

The welfare system began in the 1930s, during the Great Depression. After the Great Society legislation of the 1960s, a person who was not elderly or disabled could receive need-based aid from the federal government for the first time. Assistance included general welfare payments, healthcare through Medicaid, food stamps, special payments for pregnant women and young mothers, and federal and state housing benefits. Over 80 Federal Welfare Programs are available for those who qualify.

"The means-tested welfare system consists of 80+federal programs providing cash, food, housing, medical care, social services, training, and targeted education to aid the poor and low-income Americans"

29. Jeffrey, Terence P., "List of 80+ Federal Welfare Program", Single Mother Guide, Updated 16 February 2020, (https://singlemotherguide.com/federal-welfare-programs/).

All of them must be updated to reflect the changes in the economy. The six significant programs that must change are the ones that affect the daily life of the recipients living in poverty. I will elaborate on these topics in this chapter.

Temporary Assistance for Needy Families

Temporary Assistance for Needy Families (TANF) extends temporary financial assistance to "needy" families living on an income far below the poverty threshold. Like many social welfare programs, it was meant to be a short-term program, helping the recipient come off welfare by combining the income of employment and the subsidy of TANF, but this didn't happen. It became a lifeline, and this is the reason why.

The cap on TANF and continued growth of the Economy

The current welfare law allows a welfare recipient to receive TANF for a maximum of 60 months, although many states have adopted a shorter time limit. Thirteen states have limited TANF to 24 months or less, while only two states (just two!) have no time limit for how long you can receive TANF.

The financial assistance is granted via an Electronic Benefits Transfer Card (EBT, the more popular name everyone seems to use). It is a debit card issued to the welfare recipient, with funds disbursed on their EBT cards. They can pay their rent, daycare expenses, and even purchase food at any location that accepts the EBT card.

Each state determines how much TANF is distributed to the individual(s). Some of these States fail to understand what they are giving to the welfare recipients is unfair as the cost of living continues to rise. In contrast, other States notice that the welfare recipient's financial assistance should be as the economy grows. TANF cash benefits vary significantly from State to State. For a family of three, the maximum TANF benefit paid in 2018 ranged from $170 per month in Mississippi to $1,039 per month in New Hampshire—the most generous of any State.

LEAST GENEROUS STATES	MAXIMUM BENEFITS
Mississippi	$170
Tennessee	$185
Arkansas	$204
Alabama	$215
Louisiana	$240
Kentucky	$262
North Carolina	$272
Arizona	$278
Georgia	$280

Benefits for a family of three are *below 30%* of the poverty line in 33 states and the District of Columbia, with 18 of those states paying *less than_20%* of the poverty line—less than $400 a month for a single person mother of two. If the government says you qualify for TANF, why is the State regulating how much you need? I believe the government should set the rate, and the States should distribute financial assistance.

How does the SNAP (Supplemental Nutrition Assistance Program) benefit the poor?

"SNAP is a federal program that helps millions of low-income Americans put food on the table. Across the United States, there are 9.5 million families with children on SNAP. It is the largest program working to fight hunger in America"

30. "Understanding SNAP, the Supplemental Nutrition Assistance Program," Feeding America, (https://www.feedingamerica.org/take-action/advocate/federal-hunger-relief-programs/snap).

Formally known as the Family Nutrition Program and Food Stamp Nutrition Education in 1988, and was renamed SNAP on 1 October 2008. Everyone is entitled to SNAP benefits, with no discrimination tolerated, but you must meet the requirements, and your income must be in or below the federal poverty level.

There is a work requirement with SNAP enrollment. You must work at least 30 hours a week; if you are of ages 16-59, you cannot voluntarily quit and reduce your work hours to below 30 hours a week without a good reason. There are exceptions to the SNAP program regarding poverty-stricken individuals. Work requirements are waivered for the following:

- Already working at least 30 hours a week (or earning wages at least equal to the federal minimum wage multiplied by 30 hours)
- Meeting work requirements for another program (TANF or unemployment compensation)
- Taking care of a child under six or an incapacitated person
- Unable to work due to a physical or mental limitation
- Participating regularly in an alcohol or drug treatment program
- Studying in school or a training program at least part-time

What is the downside of applying for SNAP?

SNAP is a federally funded program; the individual states determine the amount distributed according to their guidelines. Using Illinois as an example, the maximum monthly income you can have and be eligible for SNAP are as detailed:

Number of People in Your Household	Maximum Gross Monthly Income	Maximum Gross Monthly Income (Age 60 and Over or Disabled)
1	$ 1,718	$ 2,082
2	$ 2,326	$ 2,818
3	$ 2,933	$ 3,555
4	$ 3,541	$ 4,292
5	$ 4,149	$ 5,028
6	$ 4,757	$ 5,765
7	$ 5,364	$ 6,502
8	$ 5,972	$ 7,238
9	$ 6,580	$ 7,975
10	$ 7,188	$ 8,712

And this is what SNAP will provide as a benefit if you meet the income requirements:

Number of People in Your Household	Maximum Gross Monthly Benefits
1	$ 194
2	$ 355
3	$ 509
4	$ 646
5	$ 768
6	$ 921
7	$ 1,018

Number of People in Your Household	Maximum Gross Monthly Benefits
8	$ 1,164
9	$ 1,310
10	$ 1,456

The Problem with SNAP

Continuing the Illinois model, how do you expect a household to survive on $194.00 a month from SNAP benefits? Maybe the people overseeing SNAP need to go grocery shopping for an entire month with a budget of $194.00. They wouldn't make it to week two! Let's look at this website called the people history website (the peoplehistory.com). Since SNAP (formally known as the Food Stamps Program) changed its name in the '90s, let's see what groceries cost. The people's history website explains the cost of food from a different era of time. We are reviewing the '80s for our example:

Reference #30.
http://www.thepeoplehistory.com/90sfood.html#:~:text=these%20are%20some%20of%20the,cents%20per%20pound%20pennsylvania%201981)

Groceries as Priced in the '90s

Apples 99 cents per pound New Jersey 1996

Apples 99 cents per pound Wisconsin 1998

Bacon $1.24 per pound Arizona 1996

Bananas 48 cents per pound Wisconsin 1998

Bananas 45 cents per pound Washington 1999

Campbells Tomato Soup $1.00 for three cans Illinois 1991

Carrots 54 cents per pound Washington 1999

Cherries $1.47 per pound Ohio 1990

Cherries $1.70 per pound Washington 1999

Cherry Tomatoes $1.87 per pound Washington 1999

Chicken $1.05 Per pound Wisconsin 1998

Clementines $5.99 for 5 pounds New Jersey 1996

Coca Cola 99 cents for six cans New Jersey 1996

Eggs Large Grade A $1.05 per dozen Wisconsin 1998

Frankfurters $1.99 per pound New Jersey 1996

Frozen Broccoli Spears $1.35 per pound Washington 1999

Frozen Peas 97 cents per pound Washington 1999

Frozen Sweet Corn $1.03 per pound Washington 1999

Grapefruit $1.00 for 4 Ohio 1997

Ground Beef 89 cents per pound Ohio 1997

Ground Beef $1.09 Illinois 1991

Ground Chuck $1.82 per pound Wisconsin 1998

Ground Coffee $3.70 per pound Wisconsin 1998

Ketchup 96 cents per bottle New Jersey 1996

Margarine 49 cents per pound New Jersey 1996

Milk 1 gallon 99 cents Illinois 1991

Milk 1 gallon $1.90 Wisconsin 1998

Onions 69 cents for 3 pounds Ohio 1997

Oranges $1.99 for 4 pounds New Jersey 1996

Oranges 74 centas per pound Washington 1999

Peaches 79 cents per pound Pennsylvania 1998

Peppers $1.11 per pound Washington 1999

Plums 89 cents per pound Pennsylvania 1998

Pork and beans 33 cents Illinois 1991

Pork Chops $2.99 per pound Pennsylvania 1998

Pork Chops $1.98 Illinois 1991

Potatoes 31 cents per pound Washington 1999

Seedless Grapes 59 cents per pound Illinois 1991

Sirloin Steak $2.99 per pound Ohio 1997

Sliced Bacon 1.49 per pound Illinois 1991

Sliced Ham $1.99 per pound Illinois 1991

Sugar 99 cents for 5 pounds Ohio 1997

Tomatoes $1.31 per pound Wisconsin 1998

Tomatoes $1.21 per pound Washington 1999

Tuna 50 cents per can New Jersey 1996

Watermelon 12 cents per pound Illinois 1991

Watermelon 32 cents per pound Ohio 1990

Wieners $1.39 per pound Pennsylvania 1998

Data from The People History website for 2013 only provides the cost of these food items:

Dozen Eggs $1.88

Loaf of Bread $1.98

Cost of a Gallon of Gas $3.80

As you can see, the cost of groceries increased while the SNAP benefits remained the same as in the '90s. Still, think SNAP beneficiaries can buy their groceries on a $194.00 allowance? I don't think so! The need to increase SNAP benefits is relevant based on the data listed above, with lawmakers receiving input from those utilizing SNAP benefits. We need our president to put Congress to work before they take another vacation. Jeez!

Medicaid/Medicare: What is the Difference? How are lower Income Individuals and Families are Covered?

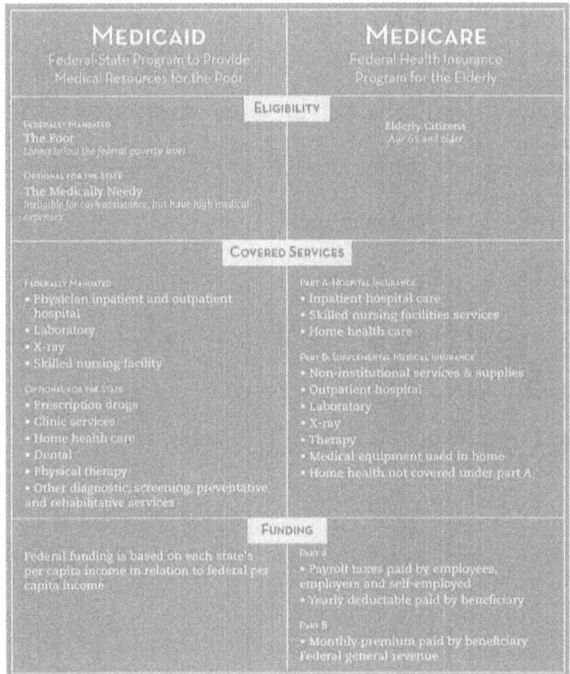

MEDICAID Federal-State Program to Provide Medical Resources for the Poor	MEDICARE Federal Health Insurance Program for the Elderly
ELIGIBILITY	
FEDERALLY MANDATED The Poor *Living below the federal poverty level* OPTIONAL FOR THE STATE The Medically Needy *Ineligible for cash assistance, but have high medical expenses*	Elderly Citizens *Age 65 and older*
COVERED SERVICES	
FEDERALLY MANDATED • Physician inpatient and outpatient hospital • Laboratory • X-ray • Skilled nursing facility OPTIONAL FOR THE STATE • Prescription drugs • Clinic services • Home health care • Dental • Physical therapy • Other diagnostic, screening, preventative and rehabilitative services	PART A: HOSPITAL INSURANCE • Inpatient hospital care • Skilled nursing facilities services • Home health care PART B: SUPPLEMENTAL MEDICAL INSURANCE • Non-institutional services & supplies • Outpatient hospital • Laboratory • X-ray • Therapy • Medical equipment used in home • Home health not covered under part A
FUNDING	
Federal funding is based on each state's per capita income in relation to federal per capita income	PART A • Payroll taxes paid by employees, employers and self-employed • Yearly deductable paid by beneficiary PART B • Monthly premium paid by beneficiary Federal general revenue

Medicare is a federal program that offers health insurance to American citizens and other eligible individuals. The requirements of Medicare are simple: you must be 65 or older; you can apply if you are with a disability; age is not an issue if you are diagnosed with end-stage renal disease or amyotrophic lateral sclerosis (ALS). There are various plans from Parts A+B, Parts A+B plus D prescription coverage, Parts A+B plus Medicare supplemental plan, Parts A + B plus both Part D prescription coverage, and a Medicare supplement plan. And there's Medicare Advantage Part C with no drug coverage, Part C with built-in Part D prescription coverage, and Part C plus a standalone Part D prescription coverage plan in limited circumstances.

Medicare is not for the lower-income communities because these plans cost more than the lower-income families and individuals can afford. Many Medicare plans charge premiums—a fixed amount that you pay monthly for your coverage.

You also pay a share of the cost for healthcare services you receive. There are three types of payments you may have:

Deductible: A set amount you pay out of pocket for covered services each year before Medicare or your plan begins to pay.

Copay: A fixed amount you pay at the time you receive a covered service. For example, you might pay $20 when you visit the doctor or $12 when you fill a prescription.

Coinsurance: A percentage of the cost for a covered service that you pay when you receive it. For example, Medicare might pay 80% of the covered service, and you would pay the remaining 20%.

31. "Medicare101:HowMedicareWords",HelloMedicare,(https://hellomedicare.com/medicare-101/?CustomFMO1=HM000337&CustomTrack2=8884896276&hellomedicare_launch_aug2018&ppc&bing&nonbrand&what%20is%20medicare&gclid=d4711be397c015dc56fc453f78ee459d&gclsrc=3p.ds&msclkid=d4711be397c015dc56fc453f78ee459d&utm_source=bing&utm_medium=cpc&utm_campaign=ba-uhg-hm-nonbrand-influencers&utm_term=what%20is%20medicare&utm_content=early-medicare).

What do we know about Medicaid?

The name implies a form of "medical-aid" or "entitlement program" that provides free or low-cost health care coverage to more than 65 million children, pregnant women, and people with disabilities. Before the ACA (Affordable Care Act), Medicaid provided services for children, parents, pregnant women, seniors, and people with disabilities. On 23 March 2010, the ACA (Affordable Care Act) changed this. Now, any adult between 19 and 65 with income below the predetermined threshold is eligible.

Now for the sad news. 17 States did not expand Medicaid under the new guidelines of the ACA. Instead, they kept the eligibility threshold to 43% or about $9,000 for a single mother of two, with only two states—

Tennessee and Wisconsin—covering parents with incomes at or near poverty.

32. ("Medicaid," Single Mother Guide, Updated 7 February 2020, https://singlemotherguide.com/medicaid-health-insurance-for-the-poor/).

Why are these prescriptions not covered under Medicaid?

Our current lawmakers need to revise the prescription list not covered under Medicaid. Specific prescriptions such as weight loss/gain medication, when successful, change the cost of additional long-term healthcare for other conditions experienced by the individual.

These are but a few of the prescriptions and services not covered by Medicaid:

- Weight loss or weight gain medications
- Medications used to treat cold or cough symptoms
- Fertility medications
- Vitamins and minerals (except prenatal vitamins or fluoride preparation products)
- Medications used for hair growth or cosmetic reasons
- Medications used to treat sexual dysfunction (unless used to treat a condition other than sexual dysfunction)
- Prescription drugs and other products not covered by TRICARE (Military Health Insurance—can you believe this?)

- Drugs used to treat a non-covered condition
- Drugs prescribed for cosmetic purposes
- Homeopathic and herbal preparations
- Fluoride preparations

Poverty-stricken individuals or families have the right to decide what is needed to improve their quality of living. We know at the end of the day, the denials of certain medications are about money being made and saved, only to be diverted to other programs such as foreign aid, special interest groups, or the beautification of the wealthy communities. The money must come from somewhere; you might as well take it from the poor.

It is strengthening the Affordable Care Act, making it stronger and beneficial to Americans?

President Obama's legacy lives on through his work to provide affordable healthcare for those who cannot afford to pay the premiums associated with healthcare insurances. On 23 March 2010, President Obama signed the (ACA) into law (also referred to as Obamacare). With one stroke of a pen, 11.8 million people, not covered by their employers, and the individuals who made less than 138% of the poverty line were covered with affordable healthcare insurance. People no longer rely on long sits in the emergency room or the "free clinics" for health care. The

ACA is the first of its kind, and we can build on its foundation to make it better!

How does the Affordable Care Act work?

The ACA opened the door for uninsured Americans to "shop" for healthcare insurances that fit their individual(s) and medical needs. The provisions of different health plans available under the ACA provide:

- The layout of the online marketplace (known as the ACA Healthcare Exchange) where individuals and business owners can shop for coverage
- Instructions for applying for health insurance
- Explanation of financial penalties for those who do not obtain coverage
- Information about "coverage gaps" as they relate to state-to-state health insurance programs
- Essential considerations for uninsured health coverage shoppers as with any healthcare insurance, the ACA made sure certain benefits were considered necessary and excluded from the ACA.
- Ambulatory patient services
- Emergency services
- Hospitalization
- Maternity and newborn care
- Mental health and substance abuse disorder services (including behavioral health treatment)

- Prescription drugs
- Rehabilitative and habilitative services (including certain devices)
- Laboratory services
- Preventive services and chronic disease management
- Pediatric services (including dental and vision)

33. "Understanding The Affordable Care Act," Medical Billing and Coding, (https://www.medicalbillingandcoding.org/health-insurance-guide/affordable-care-act/).

A Note worth mentioning for the history book on the ADA!

Had it not been for the actions of the *Maverick*, the late Republican *Senator John McCain*, who crossed his own party line and voted against the "skinny repeal" of the ACA, he killed it! He knew the needs of the many outweighed the needs of the few! I believe every person has a God-given purpose to fulfill. Senator McCain's was to stop Former President Trump and his Administration from taking away healthcare from 11.8 million people. He rode off into the sunset, knowing he had accomplished his mission! Job well done! May you rest in peace!

Healthcare insurance companies are still swinging!

The ACA needs improvement because of the healthcare insurance companies and their stranglehold on physicians' ability to care for their patients. A physician can only send their recommendation to the insurance company for approval to perform a procedure. The insurance companies still retain the final authority to override the physician's request. And to think, the physician knew what was best for their patient?

Making ACA Better, Faster, and a Stronger Affordable Health Care Insurance

What can our government do to upgrade the ACA? Think about the patients and take it to the next level by doing the following:

1. Guarantee no patient will undergo a life-saving procedure and incur any out-of-pocket expenses.
2. Guarantee life-saving prescriptions for illnesses such as cancer, diabetes, ALS, MS, dementia, and others will be covered 100% by the healthcare insurance companies.
3. Cover products like diabetic shoes or other prostheses to enhance patients' lives will be covered 100% by healthcare insurance companies.
4. Provide coverage for chiropractic care at no cost to the patient.
5. Guarantee herbal medicine and treatments will be covered in all healthcare insurance plans.

From what we know of history, the moment the wheel was invented, there has always been a continuous process of making one better and more durable until we have what is known as the tire today. Obamacare should not be the end-all-be-all for people who normally could not afford healthcare insurance, but the insurance is ready to go to the following healthcare level. Let's make it better!

Chapter 5

Does Poverty Discriminate?

The U.S. Census Bureau completed it's 2018 "People in Poverty by Selected Characteristics." The one thing everyone seems to get right is this: Poverty does not discriminate. View the column to the left and the first column to the right to fully understand poverty by selected characteristics.

34. Jessica Semega, Melissa Kollar, John Creamer, and Abinash Mohanty, "Income and Poverty in the United States: 2018", census.gov, September 2019, (https://www.census.gov/data/tables/2019/demo/income-poverty/p60-266.html)

People in Poverty by Selected Characteristics: 2018

Characteristic	Poverty Levels for 2018			
	Below Poverty			
	Number	Margin of error[2] (+/-)	Percent	Margin of error[2] (+/-)
PEOPLE				
Totalww	**38,146**	**791**	**11.8**	**0.2**
Race and Hispanic Origin				
White..	24,945	615	10.1	0.2
White, not Hispanic..............................	15,725	453	8.1	0.2
Black..	8,884	416	20.8	1.0
Asian..	1,996	157	10.1	0.8
Hispanic (any race)................................	10,526	403	17.6	0.7
Sex				
Male...	16,782	428	10.6	0.3
Female..	21,363	462	12.9	0.3
Age				
Under age 18...	11,869	415	16.2	0.6
Aged 18 to 64..	21,130	479	10.7	0.2
Aged 65 and older..................................	5,146	206	9.7	0.4

Nativity				
Native-born	31,828	713	11.4	0.3
Foreign-born	6,317	283	13.8	0.6
Naturalized citizen	2,215	147	9.9	0.6
Not a citizen	4,103	227	17.5	0.8
Region				
Northeast	5,682	304	10.3	0.6
Midwest	7,005	378	10.4	0.6
South	16,757	573	13.6	0.5
West	8,701	420	11.2	0.5
Residence				
Inside metropolitan statistical areas	31,936	771	11.3	0.3
Inside principal cities	15,287	609	14.6	0.5
Outside principal cities	16,649	615	9.4	0.3
Outside metropolitan statistical areas	6,210	526	14.7	0.8
Work Experience				
Total, aged 18 to 64	21,130	479	10.7	0.2
All workers	7,781	256	5.1	0.2
Worked full-time, year-round	2,544	133	2.3	0.1
Less than full-time, year-round	5,237	213	12.7	0.5
Did not work at least 1 week	13,349	354	29.7	0.7

Disability Status				
Total, aged 18 to 64	21,130	479	10.7	0.2
With a disability	3,818	186	25.7	1.1
With no disability	17,279	391	9.5	0.2
Educational Attainment				
Total, aged 25 and older	21,916	440	9.9	0.2
No high school diploma	5,693	222	25.9	0.9
High school, no college	7,925	255	12.7	0.4
Some college	4,812	183	8.4	0.3
Bachelor's degree or higher	3,486	214	4.4	0.3

The Link between Mental Illness and Poverty

"In 2016, The Substance Abuse and Mental Health Services Administration (SAMHSA) released a report about the association between mental health disorders and poverty. The report indicated that 9.8 million adults in the United States had a serious mental illness in 2015. Nearly 25 percent of these individuals were living below the poverty line."

35. (Gonzales, Matt, "Mental Illness and Poverty: A Depressing Reality," The Recovery Village, 9 November 2019, https://www.therecoveryvillage.com/mental-health/related/mental-illness-and-poverty/).

The climate of the Southside of Chicago teaches you to be very observant of your surroundings. I know this because I was born and raised there. One observation forever burned in my memory is the look of despair. I often wondered why some of the older people walking down the street would always have this petrified look on their faces. Later in life, I would learn what a depressed, miserable, and void of hope look like. How could that be?

Parents living in poverty have that one character trait they would never relinquish: the willingness to sacrifice for their children. Only the child who made it out of the slums remembers the parent who sacrificed their dream to become great. No one talks about the parent that always smiles when their life is crumbling around them. When buying sports equipment means going without new shoes.

When paying for training means giving up that much-needed vacation. Working two jobs ensures your child is equipped with the right tools to escape the poverty-stricken community. The toll this sacrifice takes on the parents is shocking. Parents deserve to live their dreams too. When your child is revealed to the world and reaches their pinnacle of success, what's left for the parents to do with their life?

When the celebrations are over, the parents let their guard down, and we see the person's reflection in the mirror; we discover they are not the same anymore. The cost of helping your child reach the pinnacle of success is shocking. On the inside, the parents struggle with the mental aspects of learning to live a new life as survivors.

They are battle-weary, depressed, broken, and trying to put the pieces of their life back together, so people will stop staying, "That is the mother of (famous person)" when they should say, "That is Ms. (person with their own identity). Parents do not get the credit they deserve to shield their children from the severe mental illnesses of growing up in poverty.

Understanding the Vice Grip Mental Illness Has on Poverty-Stricken People

Poverty is just the outer shell, and mental illness is the anomaly, the soul eater that destroys the individual(s) with 98% accuracy. We spent all our resources making sure poverty doesn't grasp our children, only to discover it was after us all this time!

If you did not live your goals in life, it was successful. When you give up your dreams, even to help your children achieve theirs, something happens to the parent on the inside. They lose their identity and what God had in store for them to accomplish in life. Poverty with mental illness is a formidable combination that no one can defeat alone.

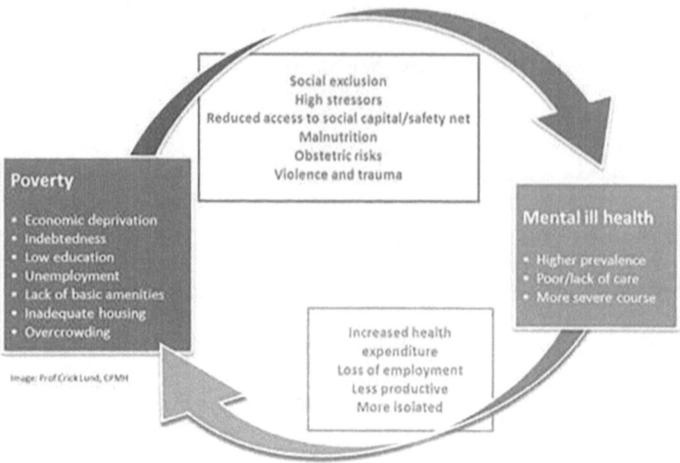

This chart showed the treacherous cycle of poverty and mental illness. We are led to believe this is an unbreakable cycle from poverty to mental illness and back to poverty and so on, but this is not true. As the illustration shows, there is a small opening between the poverty–mental illness loop. That same opening can be used to develop programs to aid those suffering from mental illness and poverty. I will discuss ideas for overcoming this stigma.

Battling mental illness is a challenge for people living in poverty. While the government has various programs to help them survive in poor conditions, the one program not made available to the poor is mental health treatment. Many people do not understand that the physiological scars poverty leaves on its victims. PTSD is one of the many mental illnesses experienced by people living in poverty with little or no treatment. Hopefully, this will change with a new administration and POTUS.

The need for mental health services expansion for the Poor

We need to expand the number of mental health facilities in the United States. "708 psychiatric hospitals and 5220 outpatient mental health facilities for 40 million adults 18 years and older are insufficient."

36. Frederic Michas, "Mental health facilities by type of facility in the U.S. 2019, statista.com, October 20, 2020, https://www.statista.com/statistics/712614/mental-health-facilities-number-in-the-us-by-facility-type/#:~:text=Mental%20health%20facilities%20are%20critically%20important%20for%20treating,that%20year%20with%20just%20708%20facilities%20in%20total.

"Depression is the leading cause of disability worldwide. Almost 75% of people with mental disorders remain untreated in developing countries with almost 1 million people taking their lives each year. In addition, according to the World Health Organization (WHO), 1 in 13 globally suffers from anxiety. The WHO reports that anxiety disorders are the most common mental disorders worldwide with specific phobia, major depressive disorder, and social phobia being the most common anxiety disorders."

Reference no. 37.
(https://adaa.org/understanding-anxiety/facts-statistics#:~:text=Facts%20%26%20Statistics.%20Advertisement.%20Anxiety%20disorders%20are%20the,yet%20only%2036.9%25%20of%20those%20suffering%20receive%20treatment.)

If you don't believe poverty affects mental health, read this, "Someone doesn't know how damaging poverty is until they have personally felt its effects. Struggling to pay bills and provide enough food puts pressure on millions of families each year. The effects of poverty can follow a child into adulthood, leading to chronic illness and lack of education or the ability to work."

38. "The Effects of Poverty," Moveforhunger.org, https://moveforhunger.org/the-effects-of-poverty. Accessed on 10/16/2021.

"There is also a wide range of negative psychological effects caused by poverty. Children are at a greater risk of behavioral and emotional problems, which could include impulsiveness, difficulty getting along with peers, aggression, attention-deficit/hyperactivity disorder, and conduct disorder. Parents may face chronic symptoms from the effects of poverty like stress and depression. Married couples may also feel marital distress and exhibit tougher parenting behaviors." If 75% of people are not being treated for mental illness, you have to wonder what type of lifestyle they are living?

Sufficient mental health facilities will "free up" correctional facilities used to maintain and treat the mentally ill, who are often their own worst enemy when they refuse to take their medication.

The government needs to pass laws requiring all insurances companies to provide 100% coverage for mental illness, with no exceptions.

What Is the Relationship between Living in Poverty and Incarceration?

"Poor people, especially people of color, face a far greater risk of being fined, arrested, and even incarcerated for minor offenses than white Americans. A broken taillight, an unpaid parking ticket, a minor drug offense, sleeping on a sidewalk, or a park bench could result in you doing jail time."

39. Dolan, Karen, "The Poor Get Prison: The Alarming Spread of the Criminalization of Poverty," Institute for Policy Studies, 18 March 2015, (https://ips-dc.org/the-poor-get-prison-the-alarming-spread-of-the-criminalization-of-poverty/).

Why do the impoverished spend more time in the correctional system than the middle- or upper-class social communities combined?

The correlation between poverty and crimes leading to incarceration is depressing. Try earning a standard of living with no education, a job that pays below minimum wage, unable to buy the necessities for daily living such as food, clothing, a roof over your head. These are all the ingredients for committing crimes. When you and your family live in poverty, someone is willing to take the risks of resorting to stealing to survive. The middle and upper classes do not understand living in poverty: When you have nothing to lose for trying to put food on your table. You develop a "survive by any means necessary" attitude, including the willingness to be incarcerated, so your family goes to bed with a full belly.

Committing crimes is the number one reason someone is incarcerated. The second reason they remain incarcerated before trial is the legal system. People of poverty and color are treated harsher by the judicial process than the middle and upper-class incarcerated. How does the legal system keep poverty-stricken people confined?

Many people are in local jails because they cannot afford to pay bail.

Solution: If the crime is nonviolent, the bail should be according to the offender's income.

Prisoners are laborers for the private prisons and the state. Keeping them incarcerated until a court date is given allows this free labor to continue. Think about that the next time you see people picking up your thrown trash on the highway. For some of them, their crime is simply not able to pay their bail.

Solution: Don't utilize nonviolent criminals pending a court date because they couldn't pay bail!

Repeat offenders. How is the justice system at fault for this? They are not, but the government is.

Solution: Deal with the issues causing the criminal events. It's easy to convict someone for stealing but never to deal with the reason why. In poverty-stricken communities, there are many reasons why people commit crimes, except murder. We need to deal with the issues!

Poverty-stricken people can't afford decent attorneys, and they are assigned a public defender. The state pays public defenders. They already have a chip on their shoulder for not being able to bill you. Also, they don't care if you are sentenced or vindicated, and for that reason, they won't give you 100% of themselves. Their job is to fulfill the Constitution by making sure you're represented by law.

Solution: Hire private attorneys and pay them to be public defenders. Besides a case-by-case salary, forfeit the right to tax them for each case they labor for the state as a public defender.

Chapter 6

Why can't the poor survive on SSI?

As if being poor wasn't enough, try surviving on SSI income. It's worse than living paycheck to paycheck because you can't earn a living due to a disability that prevents you from working for a living. The plight of the poor is just intensified by your lack of income and the struggle to pay your bills. SSI is supposed to rectify this problem, but real-life testimonies tell a different story of the desperate need for the SSI program to be updated to coincide with the rising cost of the economy.

People on SSI are poor. They make up 38-40 percent of the poverty rate for SSI recipients. There is no extra funding for luxurious living, vacations, dining out, buying fashionable clothing, or purchasing items we take for granted, like a flat-screen TV. If there were a comparison of SSI and a floatation device, SSI would drown. There are too many restrictions with the SSI program to prevent people from living comfortably while receiving SSI benefits.

What do we know about SSI?

SSI is both a blessing and a curse. The benefit is its' something, but the curse is it isn't enough. President Nixon signed the Social Security Amendments of 1972 on October 30, 1972, which created the SSI Program. Supplemental Security Income (SSI) is a federal income supplement program funded by general tax revenues (not Social Security taxes):

- It is designed to help aged, blind, and disabled people who have little or no income; and
- It provides cash to meet basic needs for food, clothing, and shelter.

SSI amounts for 2021

Like most government programs, SSI doesn't provide enough to support basic needs. The monthly maximum Federal amounts for 2021 are $794 for an eligible individual, $1,191 for a qualified individual with an eligible spouse, and $397 for an essential person. The government expects you to live off their generous SSI benefits minus the cost of utilities, rent, food, and lifestyle expenses. But wait, it gets better. If your disability allows you to work, your SSI benefit can be reduced based on the federal benefit rate. (See chart below for example.)

EXAMPLE B – SSI Federal Benefit with only
EARNED INCOME ____________

Total monthly income = $317 (Gross wages)

1) $317 (Gross wages)

-20 (Not counted)

$297

-65 (Not counted)

= $232 divided by 1/2 =$116 (Countable income)

2) $794 (SSI Federal benefit rate)

-116(Countable income)

=$678 (SSI Federal benefit)

40. https://www.ssa.gov/ssi/text-income-ussi.htm

For this reason, the honest poverty-stricken people work "under the table." The system is designed to keep them in poverty; while most debtors are sympathetic to your situation, they expect to be paid in full, or there goes your credit!

How does the poor survive on SSI?

If your disability or age prevents you from working and SSI is the only source of income for poverty-stricken people, there are ways you can survive on SSI. People have been doing this for years because it's all about survival.

Apply for Section 8 Housing. Rent is income-based, regardless of the number of rooms in the apartment or Section 8 house—next, food stamps. It's $200 per person in most states, but this isn't true. One single mother I consulted with said she receives $35.00 in food stamps. Who can live on $35.00 worth of food stamps per month? There is no explanation for this lack of compassion towards people, especially those suffering.

Should your disability be worse than most on SSI benefits, the state will pay someone to provide Home Aide to tend to your needs. Most of the time, it's a family member or someone you know. When you are at the point, a family member can no longer care for you, off you go to the nursing home!

Not everyone receives the same amount of SSI. One person I interviewed told me they received less than $700.00 per month, despite the physician telling SSI that they should never work or drive a vehicle again due to their disability. What do you do? There are ways you can make the SSI benefits work along with other subsidy programs.

One of these programs is called the low-income Home Energy Assistance Program (LIHEAP). This program allows low-income individuals and their families assistance with their utility payments. To qualify, your annual income must be a certain percentage below the federal poverty level. The funds go directly to the utilities. If your bills are outstanding, the grant will pay your entire balance so you can start the new year in a clean state.

Questions from someone living on SSI

If you are on SSI, you're probably thinking the same questions as the person I interviewed about the SSI program.

1. We don't get paid enough SSI; why penalize us for finding a "piece of a job?"
2. Why Section 8 isn't part of the SSI program. Everyone can't afford to pay the total amount for rent.
3. How come the food stamp program isn't part of the SSI program. I receive $35.00 for food stamps. How much do groceries cost?

Takeaways that would revamp the SSI program

Like most government programs, the SSI program needs to catch up with the rise in living costs. Here are a few suggestions that are a start to revamping the SSI program.

1. Flip the Benefits payment to $1,191 for the individual and an extra $794 for the eligible spouse.
2. Pay all SSI Recipients the same SSI Benefit regardless of their disability.
3. Add "food stamps" as an SSI benefit.

4. Stop penalizing people with a bit of saving or checking accounts. Everyone has the right to try to climb out of a financial hole; besides, the average person living in poverty is living paycheck to paycheck.

Perhaps the most significant overhaul to the SSI program is conducting a periodic town hall meeting with the SSI recipients and asking them what they need. Listen to their stories of survival with SSI benefits as their only source of income. Then change the system to reflect their needs and not look good on the news; knowing what the government does is not enough.

Chapter 7

How about we use some of our Foreign Aid funding to help OUR poor?

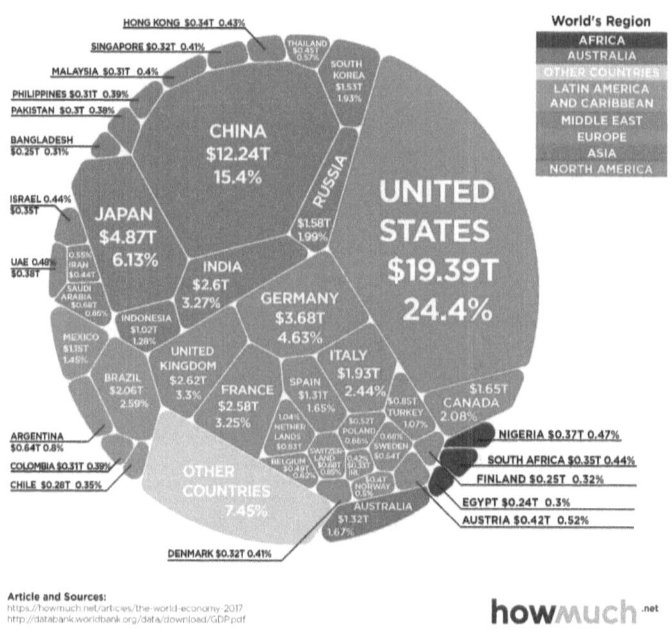

"The American taxpayer has been generous to foreign countries. Between 2013 and 2018, nearly $300 billion in U.S. taxpayer money flowed as "aid" to countries outside the United States. Each year, the U.S. spends about $47 billion. Half the aid went to Africa and the Middle East in FY2018, the latest year available for these statistics."

41. Andrezejewski, Adam, "New Report: Nearly $300 Billion In Foreign Aid Spent By U.S. Government," forbes.com, 8/4/2021, https://www.forbes.com/sites/adamandrzejewski/2021/08/04/new-report-nearly-300-billion-in-foreign-aid-spent-by-us-government/?sh=2f88f3a34374. Assessed on 10/16/2021.

$47 billion? To foreign aid? While Americans struggle to put food on their table and gas in their cars? "When the American people are asked what government spending should be cut in order to balance the federal budget, foreign aid programs generally top the list."

U.S. TOP 10 FUNDED INTERNATIONAL ORGANIZATIONS FY2019

RANK	INTERNATIONAL ORGANIZATION	U.S. CONTRIBUTION FY2019
1	WORLD FOOD PROGRAM	$3 BILLION
2	UN HIGH COMMISSIONER FOR REFUGEES	$2 BILLION
3	GLOBAL (AIDS) FUND	$849 MILLION
4	UN CHILDREN'S FUND	$673 MILLION
5	NATO	$625 MILLION
6	INTERNATIONAL ORGANIZATION OF MIGRATION	$572 MILLION
7	INTERNATIONAL COMMITT ON RED CROSS	$474 MILLION
8	UN (DIRECT)	$463 MILLION
9	WORLD HEALTH ORGANIZATION	$421 MILLION
10	UN Mission in the Republic of South Sudan	$310 MILLION

Source: OpenTheBooks.com analysis of State Dept. data in U.S. Contributions to International Organizations, 2019 Report, September 15, 2020. Learn more at OpenTheBooks.com

Why do we provide so much foreign aid to others when we have 34 million living in poverty at home? The advantages and disadvantages of foreign aid take a look at the reality of this transfer of wealth. The average American believes 25% of the government's budget goes to foreign aid. The fact is, about 1% of the budget is directly associated with this practice.

42. Gaille, Brandon, "21 Advantages and Disadvantages of Foreign Aid", BrandonGaille, 27 February 2018, (https://brandongaille.com/21-advantages-disadvantages-foreign-aid/)

It creates a positive back-and-forth relationship.

The United States regularly receives Foreign Aid, just as it regularly hands it out. Russia donated over 60 tons of supplies in the aftermath of Hurricane Katrina. The United Arab Emirates has built a neonatal facility in Missouri and donated Apple computers to local students. Turkey provided Foreign Aid to the U.S. for clean drinking water in a remote area of Oregon. Even Kenya once donated 14 cows as an act of goodwill after the events of 9/11. With foreign aid, what goes around typically comes around.

It can Save Lives.

Foreign Aid is offered when there is a national emergency in another country. That may be due to an earthquake, a hurricane, a volcanic eruption, or some other natural disaster type. It provides a way to help people access food and clean water supplies when they may have zero access to those supplies for an extended time. Once the basics are provided, people can focus on being able to rebuild their lives. In many ways, Foreign Aid is the first step toward the hope that can be found during the process of starting over after a disaster hit.

It stops the effects of poverty.

Foreign Aid allows developing countries to access food, water, and shelter resources that they may normally not have. Billions of people live on $2 per day or less. The cost to feed these people is often less than $0.25 per meal. By working to eliminate poverty, providing nations can develop new resources in the countries that receive aid so that everyone can benefit somehow.

It benefits the Country by providing Foreign Aid.

"Providing help during a time of need is more than merely good ethics. It is also good politics. Foreign Aid encourages positive diplomatic relationships. It can create new job opportunities, trade agreements, and even better security arrangements. Although providing Foreign Aid is a direct cost that taxpayers from the providing nation bear, numerous rewards come from such an action that isolationism could never provide."

Changing our Foreign Aid Policy to better America!

Stop giving countries what they ask for; they are the borrowers. Instead, give them what is considered reasonable. It would be nice if the United States would adopt a policy that limits the amount we provide to each country. I know we have U.N. obligations, but it's time these same nations recognize OUR need to take care of OUR people.

Takeaways the U.S. can benefit using some of the Foreign Aid Funding

1. Increase employment-too many people are unemployed for all the wrong reasons. The jobs available don't pay enough to quiet the bill collectors. As the economy rises, so should minimum wage.
2. Sustain welfare programs-there is hardly talk on Capitol Hill about increasing the social welfare programs. Now is a great time to help our poor become profitable and presentable, throwing a lifeline to millions of Americans living in poverty.
3. Invest in high-quality childcare/education-everyone knows that poverty-stricken people children receive the worst education and childcare in the nation. By providing more funding for childcare and education, poverty-stricken people will have equality in advancing their livelihood.
4. Tackle segregation and concentrated poverty- you can't tackle what you won't admit exists. Segregation of races in poverty-

stricken communities ensures there will always be a lower-class to work for the wealthy.

5. Invest in adult education- a higher level of education means promotions. The problem is the majority of the adults living in poverty can't afford to return to school, and they don't qualify for bank loans. Make education for adults returning to the workforce free and have corporations foot the bill for higher learning of their employees seeking advancement in their career field.
6. Devote funds to the beautification of impoverished communities. No one wants to stare out the window and see burned-down homes, abandoned and boarded-up apartment buildings—drug dealers on every corner, liquor, and cigarette/ vaper advertisements all over the community. Improving the image of the impoverished goes a long way with someone's mental state of being.
7. Improving the quality of housing for the poor-you can't move everyone to the suburbs, including the poor. Building affordable housing and tearing down "eyesore" homes to improve the community's image and at no expense of the tenant or owner.

The federal government argues that this aid is necessary to maintain reasonable diplomatic relations, assist allies, and encourage pro-American sentiment abroad. No one is disputing the discontinuation of helping other countries during their time of need. We are arguing this; if we have enough funding to contribute to foreign aid, there shouldn't be not one family going hungry in America. Not one unemployed person, and communities not impoverished. Let's take care of our needy before we open our pocketbooks to others in need.

Chapter 8

Serving our Active Duty Servicemembers as they serve Us!

Like the caption reads, "We owe them all." Why? Some made the ultimate sacrifice to protect this nation, while others put their dreams on hold to defend our freedom to live in a country free of fear from our government.

When I joined the U.S. Army at seventeen years old, I became part of that elite group of men and women willing to answer the call. Each branch of service required we take an oath to support and defend the interest of this nation, with expectations of being taken care of just as they did. Did America live up to its end of the deal, taking care of active-duty servicemembers?

"About 23,000 active duty personnel received benefits from the Supplemental Nutrition Assistance Program (SNAP, previously food stamps) in 2013, the latest year for which statistics are available. This is a lower percentage than hunger rates for the average U.S. household (2 percent versus 12.3 percent). However, no one helping to defend our country should struggle to put food on the table."

43. Fact Sheet: Hunger and Poverty in the Military Community, bread.org, 7/20/2018, https://bread.org/library/fact-sheet-hunger-and-poverty-military-community. Accessed on 10/17/2021.

What is the government doing about making sure no one helping to defend our nation should struggle to put food on their table?

WIC (Women, Infant, and Children) supports servicemembers

"This week, the White House proposed a $17 billion budget cut to the Supplemental Nutrition Assistance Program, which helps millions of low-income Americans feed themselves and their families. An estimated

23,000 U.S. military families are among those who receive SNAP benefits."

44. NPR, "Military Families and SNAP Benefits," February 17, 2018, (https://www.npr.org/2018/02/17/586759930/military-families-and-snap-benefits)

When an enlistee joins the military, the majority are single, so the pay and the benefits for being a servicemember are sufficient. When they have a family or get married and have children while serving, finances are strained. The government does provide free housing and additional funding to help support your family, it's not enough because of the increase in the economy.

Servicemembers have two choices; shop at the tax-free establishments on the military installation post and pay a higher price, or shop off-post and pay what the rest of society pays plus tax. That's a hell of a trade-off for someone putting their life on the line for their nation.

If the pay of an enlistee were equivalent to someone who climbed the ranks as a Sergeant, there wouldn't be an issue, but it isn't. As long as the economy continues to rise and servicemembers' pay remains frozen, there will always be a problem. Why are service members on WIC again? Read my story.

I was an E-4 (Specialist) when my former wife gave birth to our twins. On an E-4 salary, with bills, I was advised to go to Social Services to sign up for WIC. When I received my first voucher for infant formulas, I was shocked at the amount I would've paid for baby formulas out of pocket. At $27.00 a can, once a week x 4, for a total of $108.00. I have twins, so my payment for baby formulas equaled equals up to $216.00 I would've paid from my salary. Pampers weren't included in this. What am I saying? Without WIC, servicemembers would be distraught trying to provide for their families.

What does WIC Provide?

"WIC is a government subsidy program that aims to provide healthy groceries for low-income families with children up to age 5. Pregnant or breastfeeding women can receive vouchers for healthy food like fresh produce, skim milk, eggs, wheat bread, beans, and cereal. WIC vouchers for infants can be used for formula and baby food. Children ages 1-5 will receive vouchers for fresh fruits and vegetables, milk, eggs, cheese, bread, peanut butter, tuna fish, juice, and cereal.

WIC defines low-income families as any household making less than 185% of the Federal poverty level. For a household of three people, that would mean an annual income of less than $37,167. Additional family members will raise the eligibility number, even if the other children are too old to personally qualify for WIC benefits.

Our family of six qualifies for WIC because we make less than $60,255 each year, but we only receive vouchers for our youngest child.

WIC is a separate program from SNAP, but any family that qualifies for SNAP benefits will automatically qualify for WIC as well."

45. Lightfoot, Lizann, "How WIC Benefits Military Families," the Military Wallet, 10 April 2019, (https://themilitarywallet.com/wic-benefits-military-families/).

If servicemembers spend the majority of their time worrying about their families, imagine what they think about when they are on deployments? I promise you it's not on the military mission, but the family that was left behind.

What Can Congress Do to Improve the Quality of Life for the Active-Duty Service Members?

At the lowest rank, a service member is paid $1,602 a month, plus ancillary benefits for two months, time in service while in training. Afterward, all service members are subject to promotions based on time in service and time in grade. That is not enough, especially when the service member has a family to provide for automobile payment(s), insurance, groceries, clothes for the family, etc. How much do you think is leftover from the initial $1,602? Extraordinarily little, if not none. Time for a real pay increase. They deserve it!

It's incredible how we have no problem agreeing to grant millions to a professional athlete, especially if they won the year's championship, "They earned it," we say, but a servicemember? Congress could be filibustering for years before granting a 1.5% pay increase. Are they serious? Is this how we show our service members our appreciation for what they do for our country?

What we should do for servicemembers while on active duty

- I would increase the pay of all servicemembers by $1000 per month regardless of rank.
- Tax breaks for the six months out of the year, for every year they serve!
- Provide reenlistment bonuses for everyone! No exceptions. I always thought that giving a reenlistment bonus to one service member but not others was a way of saying, "Your job is better than mine. If they are good enough to deploy, they should be entitled to a reenlistment bonus!
- Pass laws prohibiting officers and senior NCOs from discouraging service members from seeking medical treatment. This type of behavior needs to end for this reason:
    a) Servicemembers need to be treated on active duty for every injury and/or disease that occurred on active duty. Make sure it's documented in their health records.
    b) Veterans that are denied compensation benefits from the VA are the results of no documented treatment or illness in their military treatment records.

Servicemembers are loyal to this country. They are on call 24/7, and their faithfulness to serve is unparalleled to any commitment made by any other. Show them respect by taking care of their daily needs as they put their lives on the line, making The United States of America a better place to live!

Chapter 9

Save our Veterans

Veterans are people who risked their lives in the service to this county's needs. They served in one of the five branches of the armed forces and proudly wore their uniform while executing the missions of their superior officers and Congress. Do you remember them? Most of us see them in their non-glory because they have a mental illness, leading to homeless veterans. They blend in with non-homeless veterans and can be found on the street corners begging for a handout or under a bridge or overpass trying to stay warm. They have no family support.

The other Veterans with family, work and socialize with no signs to the public of desiring to end their life by committing suicide. The list below provides some reasons Veterans chose to end their life? Someone who never served would not understand. You can't until you put on that uniform and wear those boots. Some reasons Veterans commit suicide:

1. Survivor's guilt. They lived while others didn't.
2. Failure to readjust to society after living the military lifestyle for so long. a Veteran who serviced can relate their time to

being in a prison-like environment; always someone telling you when you can do just about anything. You don't snap out of it when you take the uniform off. Some never readjust.

3. Lack of employment after all they did for this country. There are no jobs for tank drivers and weapons specialists. The jobs offered are an insult to Veterans who were once in charge of equipment in the millions, and now they can't get a credible job that honors their service to our country.
4. They are depressed about their self-worth in the eyes of society. Veterans go from "thank you for your service" and all the benefits of being an active-duty servicemember to "thank you for service" followed by "get in line with the rest of the applicants."
5. Their family is afraid of living with them because they came home "different." The military will change you. Life isn't viewed like everyone else sees it. Some Veterans who see combat come home not the same as they left. Some are successful, and some aren't. Both need counseling, not abandonment from their families.

Everyone in America knows at least one Veteran, including themselves. Did you know Veterans are more prone to committing suicide than any other group in America's population?

Total Number of Veteran Suicides, 2005–2019

"Approximately 17 U.S. Veterans die by suicide every day—a rate that is about 1.5 times that of nonVeterans after adjusting for differences in age and sex, according to the Department of Veterans Affairs (VA) 2019 National Veteran Suicide Prevention Annual Report."

46. Novotney, Amy, "Stopping military and Veteran suicides" Apa.org, 1/1/2020, www.apa.org/monitor/2020/01/ce-corner-suicide. Accessed 10/2/2021.

Known statistics on Veteran's suicide-related deaths:

- The number of Veteran suicide deaths per year increased from 6,056 in 2005 to 6,399 in 2017 and 6,435 in 2018.
- The annual number of Veteran suicide deaths has exceeded 6,300 since 2008.
- The annual number of Veteran suicide deaths increased by 36 from 2017 to 2018 and by 379 from 2005 to 2018.
- The number of Veteran suicides per year was lowest in 2006 and highest in 2014, and the number in 2018 was lower than in six of the prior 13 years.

In 2005, an average of 86.6 American adults, including Veterans, died by suicide each day. There were an average of 124.4 deaths each day in 2017 and an average of 127.4 in 2018.

- Since 2005, the average number of Veteran suicide deaths per day has remained between 17 and 18, despite observed decreases in the size of the Veteran population. In 2018, an average of 17.6 Veterans died by suicide each day.

- The average of 17.6 Veteran suicide deaths per day in 2018 was higher than the 17.5 average suicide deaths per day in 2017. In 2018, the average of 17.6 Veteran suicides per day comprised 6.5 Veterans with recent VHA use and 11.1 Veterans without current VHA use.

10 Misconceptions about Suicide

Every culture experience's death related to suicide. Suicidal behavior has never been accepted, and many myths about suicide have evolved. Appropriate and effective intervention requires recognizing these myths and knowing the facts.

People often commit suicide without warning—"out of the blue."

FACT: Most people who take their lives have communicated their intent beforehand, either blatantly or subtly.

Only severely depressed people commit suicide; improvement in the emotional state means a lessened risk of suicide.

FACT: Suicide often occurs at the end of a deep depression when a person's spirits and energy level rise. Suicide requires a certain amount of energy that a severely depressed person may lack.

Suicide occurs in the greatest numbers around Christmas and Thanksgiving.

FACT: While depression is often greatest in numbers during the holiday season, suicide is highest during the spring months.

Only crazy people commit suicide.

FACT: Although most suicidal people are very unhappy, most suicidal acts are committed by people that aren't characterized as psychotic. Thus, they are generally rational and in touch with reality. Seventy-five percent of those who commit suicide are, however, clinically depressed.

If a person committed suicide, his or her situation was probably so bad that death was the best solution.

FACT: The life circumstances of suicidal individuals, while often bad, are survived by most people in similar circumstances. The perception of a challenging life circumstance is often more severe than the actual event.

People who talk about or threaten suicide don't do it.

FACT: A large percentage of people who threaten suicide carry out their threats. Take all threats seriously.

People who really want to die will find a way; it won't help to try and stop them.

FACT: Most suicidal people are highly ambivalent (unsure) about suicide. They are torn between a desire to live and a desire to die.

The tendency toward suicide is inherited and passed from generation to generation.

FACT: Since suicides often do run in families, the assumption is made that suicide is inherited. However, suicide often occurs in individuals with no family history of suicide.

One should not try to discuss suicide with depressed people. It might give them the idea or upset them enough to "push them over the edge." The best thing to do is ignore it.

FACT: Suicidal people are commonly greatly relieved to be able to talk about it.

The great majority of suicides are among minority groups in lower socioeconomic classes.

FACT: More White, middle-class, and affluent people commit suicide. However, suicide still crosses all racial/ethnic groups and classes

47. (Author Unknown, "10 Misconceptions About Suicide").

Signs of a Suicide Attempt

The two types of pain that never go away are grief and awareness. Those who were left behind are grieving. They do not understand why their loved one chose to depart this world instead of seeking help, which brings me to awareness of the second type of pain. When you find yourself saying, "How come they didn't come to me?" they may have, but you did not recognize the signs of someone crying out before they commit suicide. You should never feel disturbed over "not seeing this coming."

Even trained individuals miss a trigger (an event or a situation to happen or exist) or two. The fact that you are reading this section is an indication you want to know what to do should you come across a friend, a loved one, or a Veteran, and they start pouring their heart out to you. Listening is your first step in the right direction. Read the comments below so you will know the signs of someone that might commit suicide:

- Feeling like there is no way out.
- Anxiety, agitation, sleeplessness, or mood swings.
- Feeling like there is no reason to live.
- Rage or anger.
- Engaging in risky activities without thinking.
- Increasing alcohol or drug misuse.
- Withdrawing from family and friends.
- Thinking about hurting or killing oneself.
- Talking about death, dying, or suicide.
- Self-destructive behavior such as drug misuse, carelessly handling weapons, etc.

If you or the Veteran in your life are feeling depressed, anxious, or hopeless, or believe they are better off dead, call the VA suicide hotline number, **1-800-273-8255**, and stay with them until help arrives!

48. "2019 National Veteran Suicide Prevention Annual Report" Office of Mental Health and Suicide Prevention, U.S. Department of Veterans Affairs, (https://www.mentalhealth.va.gov/docs/data-sheets/2019/2019_National_Veteran_Suicide_Prevention_Annual_Report_508.pdf).

Chapter 10

VBA employee Woes

The Department of Veterans Administration (VA) consists of three departments, the Veterans Benefits Administration (VBA), the Veterans Health Administration (VHA), and the National Cemetery Administration (NCA). This section focuses on the VBA employees and the harsh environmental conditions they are subjected to while serving our Veterans.

The Struggles Associated with Being a VBA Employee

One aspect of poverty is that you don't have to be within the poverty level. You can be one paycheck away from losing your social status. The fear of losing everything you worked for makes you stay, but there is a toll to pay; your mental and physical health. The leaders over departments, particularly the Department of Veterans Affairs, are aware of this and failed to take action as the VBA employees express their physical and mental ailments. I'll address them for those whose voices aren't heard.

Who works for the VBA?

More than 50% of VBA employees are Veterans. The remaining employees are friends or relatives of living or deceased Veterans. VBA employees are proud of what they do, helping Veterans receive their Compensation and Pension entitlements.

Who makes the rules for the VBA employees to follow?

The taxpayers need to be aware that no one is above the government. Every VBA employee is governed by the policies created by Congress to execute their duties. Not one person within the Veterans Affairs Department, including the Under Secretary of the Department of Veterans Affairs, is exempt from following Congress's directives. VBA employees are not rogue! They are perhaps the second most loyal, hard-working, dedicated, and passionate about their job as our Servicemembers.

What you do not know about the VBA employees' woes

Every job occupation has its risk, and the VBA is no exception. The VBA employees are dedicated professionals who often come to work daily with the scars and illnesses associated with working for the VA. The physical injuries are from the longevity of employment, include:

1. Chronic headaches and migraines are related to the stress of making their daily production and quality goals, resulting in taking medication for newly diagnosed mental illnesses.
2. Always in a constant state of worry and fear of the possibility of losing their jobs for not making their products and or quality standards.
3. The stress of being overworked. More Veterans and dependents are filing claims than employees to process them, but management continually reminds the VBA employee of the importance of making our daily production.
4. Chronic arthritis in their hands, neck, and back from sitting and typing all day long.
5. Eye conditions and carpal tunnel syndrome, also job-related.
6. Fearful of losing their jobs because they can't maintain the quota established by constant-changing standards.

What can the VBA employee do? Many stay because they love what they do, while others quit with a heavy heart because it was the right thing to regain their health.

Additional burdens added by the Trump administration's change in VBA policies

Former President Trump handed down the worse actions taken against VBA employees by signing the following executive orders into law:

23 June 2017: Former President Trump signed the VA Accountability Act, granting management the authority to terminate VA employees after two pay periods of failed performance goals. That is four weeks of doing your job but not making your daily production.

Former President Trump single-handedly changed the employment status for VBA employees to the "at-will" system, meaning management no longer needed a reason for terminating a VBA employee. They can just "let you go."

25 May 2018: President Donald Trump signed three executive orders to make federal employees easier to fire while cutting back on union time. "Former President Trump signed three executive orders containing sweeping reforms that weaken protections for federal workers and eliminate perks for the unions that represent them.

Because of this change, Union presentations must occur off VA premises. They must pay rent to someone just to have a place to serve the VA employees. Also, they can't use the government email system and telephone system to speak with VA employees. Doing so would risk the VA employee and union members losing their jobs. Finally, any service provided to a VA employee must occur before or after the duty hours of the VA employee. This was ridiculous!

Former President Trump also ordered the termination of an Obama-era policy that says leniency for one worker sets a precedent protecting others from firing and shortened review periods preceding discipline for poor-performing employees.

Although these changes made it easier for workers to be fired, White House officials said they expected mostly positive responses." I bet the VA employee didn't send a "positive response."

49. (Nelson, Steven, "Trump signs three executive orders taking aims at unions," Washington Examiner, 25 May 2018, https://www.washingtonexaminer.com/news/white-house/trump-guts-union-perks-speeds-up-civil-service-firings-to-save-100-million-a-year.)

Now the good news for VBA employees

- 18 May 2020: The U.S. District Court ruled against the Trump administration, primarily striking down the executive orders, the VA rescinded its implementation of the official time order.

- Another event in 2020: The American Federation of Government Employees (AFGE) scored a major win after the appeals court ruled that the Department of Veterans Affairs had improperly applied a new law expediting an employee's removal. Former President Trump's VA Accountability and Whistleblower Protection Act is no longer valid. Employees can no longer be terminated without a Performance Improvement Plan (PIP) being implemented first. Under the Trump administration, 8,000 VA employees were fired. Now they can be hired back if they want their old jobs back with back pay.
- Management for the Department of Veterans Affairs stripped the VA Master Agreement (Rules governing the VA employees approved by Union and Management) without the Union and its members voting on this agreement.
- On Jan 22, 2021, President Biden issued Executive orders revoking his predecessors' Executive Orders 13836-Developing Efficient, Effective, and Cost-Reducing Approaches to Federal Sector Collective Bargaining- the way the Union negotiates on behalf of VA employees.
- Revoking the Executive Order 13837-Ensuring Transparency, Accountability, and Efficiency in Taxpayer-Funded Union Time Use-How the Union proved managed time with VA employees.
- Revoking the Executive Order 13839-Promoting Accountability and Streamlining Removal Procedures Consistent with Merit

System Principles- changing the system of how VA employees can be terminated.

Improving the atmosphere of the VBA will make the job asked of VBA employees easier to Execute

Listening to your employees is much better than threatening to terminate them for poor performance. Asking them what can be done to help them complete their assigned tasks is better than threatening to release them. Four comments have been circulating the VA for decades, but no one is listening. Maybe they will now.

1. How does one expect VBA employees to make their daily performance with flawed software and lagging Internet service? I have no idea how much the government spends on companies designing VA employees' programs, but they need to get a refund!

   Software programs are thrown at the VA employees to start using immediately, but the software isn't ready for use. Make the developer of software for the government test their products themselves. VA employees are not testing subjects for billion-dollar corporations standing in line to pitch their product to Congress for the VA to use.

2. Restructure the committee for developing performance standards by appointing people who work as Claim Assistants (CA), Veteran Service Representatives (VSR), Rating Veteran

Service Representatives (RVSR). Promulgation, Decision Review Officers (DRO), and Quality Management with at least five years of experience are positions they are creating standards.

VBA employees are currently working under new 2020 working performance and quality standards that are unattainable. You can't make both quality and production for each claim developed and complete the number of cases you are required to daily. No matter how fast you work, if you make your performance standards, you may get a quality error if you miss something during the development phase. No one is listening to the cries of the VA employees, especially Congress. Yet, every year we complete surveys that no one is adhering to.

3. The VA has partnered with private providers to complete compensation and pension examinations to determine if the Veterans' claim for service connection is valid. These physicians bill the government no less than $850 per exam. Many exams are returned to the examiner because they provide incomplete data. When this happens, the returned exams delay the processing of the Veteran's claim. The retraining of contract providers on how to complete a VA Disability Benefits Questionnaire (DBQ) is needed. No one is listening to the cries of the VA employees, especially Congress.
4. What happened to bonuses? For all the hard work, heartaches, and tensions the VA employees undergo to serve Veterans and

make the VA look good in front of Congress, why do some people get the bonuses while others do not? No one is listening to the cries of the VA employees, especially Congress.

VA employees should receive praises for the service they provide to the Veterans of this nation. They should have someone in Congress during senate hearings stand up for them, making the world aware that the VA employees are loyal and merely following the orders given by Congress. They are not rogue employees.

VA employees should be heard when speaking about health issues, workable equipment, and the need to improve performance and quality programs. Bonuses should be available to all employees with amounts dispersed per their performance and quality standards and additional duties performed. Finally, have the media do "feel good" stories on VA employees so the public changes their perception of the VA.

CHAPTER 11

Everyone, especially the poor wants the truth from Politicians!

No one likes being lied to, especially when you are poverty-stricken. But politicians, election after election, do this "I'll do these things when I get into power" or "I'll fight for you" speech, but never deliver. After the elections are over, so is the attention span of the politician and their promises.

The Dutch humanist Desiderius Erasmus is remembered throughout history for saying this quote: "In the land of the blind, the one-eyed man is king." Everyone will interpret this differently, but the blind man's land represents leadership in this country. You can be in charge, but if you do not know what the voter wants, you are blind. For years we listened to politicians tell us what they would do if elected. They are blind.

The one-eyed man is the king because they can see everything wrong: poverty, lack of mental health treatment and discriminatory incarceration, healthcare system, SSI, etc. Politicians think they know our needs, giving us what the press reveals to them as discussion topics. As the voter, the one-eyed man (the voter), we must show them our needs if they want us to elect/reelect them.

The Twisted Tongue of the Politician

There are reasons why politicians prefer not to tell us, the voter, the truth about their agendas. I will provide some.

50. Taylor, Jim, Ph.D., "Six Reasons Why Politicians Believe They Can Lie," Psychology Today, 24 September 2012, (https://www.psychologytoday.com/us/blog/the-power-prime/201209/six-reasons-why-politicians-believe-they-can-lie#:~:text=Ultimately,%20politicians%20lie%20because,%20due,to%20indefensible%20claims%20against%20them).

1. *Many politicians have narcissistic tendencies.* They are arrogant, self-important, see themselves as unique, require excessive admiration, have a sense of entitlement, and are exploitative. Name one politician you know that fits this description.
2. *Politicians know their followers will believe them, even in the face of irrefutable evidence to the contrary.* Politicians live in an echo chamber. Everyone watches the same news channel, listens to the same talk radio, reads the same newspapers, engages in all social media types, and hangs out with the same like-minded people.
3. *People don't want to hear the truth.* Reread #2. As the saying goes, the truth hurts, and no one wants to listen to things that

threaten their existence and beliefs or that will make them uncomfortable. It is decidedly better for politicians to tell people what makes them feel comfortable. Isn't this a takeaway from free will?

4. *Once posted on social media, it lives on forever!* Crooked politicians will use the power of social media to post bad decisions and lies about their opponents. Once the damage is done, there are no takebacks. How many politicians you know will do this to get your vote? Did a particular politician ask the Ukrainians to investigate the Democratic Presidential Candidate's son? It's on the internet.
5. *If a lie is told enough times, people will assume it is true.* It is not a stretch to understand why people will believe something if they hear it enough. People expect that lies will be disproved and fade away. So, if the lies continue to be heard, people assume they must be true.

Ultimately, politicians lie because the cost/benefit ratio for lying is in their favor. What benefit is there to deliberately deceive the people that voted for them so they can make their lives better? What can the voter do to influence the politicians to solve the problems of the impoverished?

Perks of Being a Member of Congress

The poor must convince lawmakers to adopt their agendas instead of politicians telling them what they will do when elected! Politicians gain a lot of benefits after being elected.

51. (Savitsky, Shane, "The perks of being a member of Congress" AXIOS, 28 November 2017, https://www.axios.com/the-perks-of-being-a-member-of-congress-1513307200-ba8cb415-27c0-4ee9-ac1f-f445d175bf68.html).

- Children get to attend private, well-protected schools.
- Members get annual allowances (averaging $1.27 million in the House and $3.3 million in the Senate) to staff and manage their offices almost entirely as they see fit, as well as for travel and other expenses.
- The House has averaged 138 legislative days each year since 2001, and the Senate has 162. The job requires long days, and members are often active in their districts when not in session, but how many jobs give their employees over six months to plan and schedule entirely as they see fit?
- While members of Congress are required to purchase insurance via an Affordable Care Act exchange, they receive a federal subsidy amounting to 72% of their premiums; they are also potentially eligible for lifetime health insurance under the Federal Employees Health Benefits Program upon retirement.

- Depending on age and length of service, members can receive a lifelong pension of 80%—which, given today's Congressional salary of $174,000, equals $139,200 in annual taxpayer-funded retirement benefits.
- Members of Congress have access to free, reserved parking spots at DC-area airports, a dedicated Congressional call desk with major airlines, and the ability to reserve seats on multiple flights but only pay for the flight boarded.
- Our nation's legislators get a slew of lifetime benefits even after leaving office, including a taxpayer-funded gym at the Capitol, access to the House and Senate floors, parking in House lots, and the ability to dine in the House and Senate dining rooms.

It should not come as a shock that politicians get better perks than we do for being employed at our jobs. *We wish!*

These are the perks of being poor:

a. Wondering where their next meal is coming from
b. Worrying if their job will disappear in favor of an automated facility
c. Deciding if they must buy groceries or put gas in the car for work for the week
d. Choosing where to buy new or second-hand clothes

e. Wondering if their children will overcome poverty and be successful in life
f. Worrying if their children will return home at the end of the day
g. Worrying whether their extension request to keep the utilities on will be approved
h. Hoping the landlord understands they will be short on the rent this month
i. Hoping they win the lottery, they win the Voice or American Idol, or their child makes it to a professional sports team!

Politicians are out of touch with Voters

We need our political leaders to leave their castles and visit impoverished people other than the voting season. Only when they experience the day-by-day struggles of the everyday taxpayer will they either work on what they "see" as needing replacement, torn down, or rebuilding or not care until it's time for re-election.

The choice to not re-elect Former President Trump wasn't difficult when you think of the pros and cons of living under Former President Trump and his Republican Administration. The American people simply did not want to see their lives continue to go in a downward spiral.

Change is the only *constant* in life. Yet humans are evolutionarily predisposed to resist change because of the associated risks. Despite this resistance to change, it is more important than ever that we accept change. President Bill Clinton said, "The price of doing the same old thing is far higher than the price of change." This statement is just as true today as the day he said it.

There is so much confusion among the political leaders over issues they want to give the voters instead of listening to them and giving them what they need. The division in the democratic party is at an all-time high, and the republicans Congressional and voters are taking notice of the democrat' unwillingness to use this opportunity to stand behind President Biden and his plan for this nation.

Power struggles are meaningless over poverty Struggles

With 34 million people living in impoverishment, you would think the number one agenda in American politics would be to win the war on poverty. For the first time since 2011, the Democrats control the House and the Senate. What does that mean to the working poor? It means more funding to change the landscape of poverty-stricken communities, new financing for educating adults tuition-free, and a more excellent law enforcement show of force to end the high levels of crime in the poorest of communities. That would be nice, but it's not happening, and it won't occur anytime soon. The division is the reason why.

Division in the Party

There is a great division in Congress among the Democrats. When they should be passing laws to benefit the poor and the President signing laws to make it happen, someone or some parties within the democratic congressional community aren't getting their way and aren't happy. There's one type of democrat voter, but there are five types of democrats operating on your behalf in Congress. They have splintered within their ranks, making it almost impossible to work together at a time when the Democrats control everything. These are the types of democrats you didn't know you voted for.

52. Gabriel, Brian, "Types of Democrats," theclassroom.com, 5/10/2019, theclassroom.com/types-democrats-11944.html. Assessed on 10/2/2021.

Urban Liberals

"Urban liberals" make up 29 percent of those who called themselves Democrats. These Democrats are predominantly white (73 percent) and largely female (62 percent). The majority of them live in urban areas and have an annual household income of $50,000 or more. Urban liberals support strong government regulation of business, and almost all of them (92 percent) believe there should be a high degree of separation of church and state."

Religious Democrats

"More than one-third of Democrats (34 percent) are part of a religious-identifying segment of the party. They are concentrated in the American South, and a majority of them are non-white (67 percent). Their most important political issues are continued support for major social programs, such as Social Security and Medicare, and increased government spending on job creation programs."

Agnostic Left-Wing

"There is a type of Democrat today that is part of a younger, more secular, and socially liberal demographic. The Washington Post called this type "The Agnostic Left." They are very similar to urban liberals on social issues such as support for legalized abortion and gay marriage. However, they differ considerably in their beliefs about the role of government in an individual's life and well-being: 79 percent said that people who do not "get ahead" in life have only themselves to blame; only 15 percent of urban liberals agreed with this statement."

DIY Democrats

"The Washington Post identified "Do-it-yourself" (DIY) Democrats as the smallest group of Democrats in its poll (13 percent). Only half of them called themselves "strong Democrats," and one-third of them support the Tea Party. One issue where the DIY Democrats showed strong Democrat support was raising taxes on households making $250,000 per year. They supported raising taxes on upper-middle-class families much more strongly than they supported cuts in defense spending."

Progressives

"Progressives are a complex type of Democrat who could include members from each of the different groups identified by The Washington Post poll. One of the leading progressive organizations in the United States is the Progressive Democrats of America (PDA). Founded in 2004 as a grassroots Political Action Committee working within the Democratic Party, the PDA has supported national healthcare, the protection of Social Security, and the creation of a full-employment economy by the government. Progressives also support environmental issues such charging a carbon tax and stopping global warming."

Why politicians are Lost

I promise you, I have no idea how we (the democrats) won the election with all this in-house bickering among the Democratic parties. If only they stop dividing themselves, set aside their differences, and vote for every bill to become a law to help the poor. Democrats of all parties must learn to pick their battles, agree to support the bills that they don't agree with in exchange for gaining the support of another democratic party when the time comes to support one of their bills.

This is when the Democrats can show the country, including the republicans and their voters, what they can do for America. If they only stop focusing on future elections and concentrate on why they were elected, to take care of the 34 million living in poverty. The future will take care of itself as long as you take care of the present.

Chapter 12

Final Thoughts

The 14th Dalai Lama said, "And if you can't help them, at least don't hurt them." The one desiring the POTUS position must be willing to help all living in the U.S. regardless of how they voted. This country has seen the absolute worst in humankind's behavior over the last four years, with people expressing their hate for another race, escalating to the killings of unarmed African Americans and now the attacks on Asians and Jews. In America!

There is a cry from the afflicted for our Government, our Leadership to make sweeping changes, so everyone American can advance in their social status and be treated with respect. Leadership needs to learn how to resolve the plaguing Americans without "holding back" benefits to the poorest, middle class, and upper class. Everyone needs that helping hand. It's time for Congress to bring help to all of America!

What we need from our Leadership in Congress

1. Come up with a strategy to fix what's broken in America without prejudice.
2. Fund higher level education at the expense of the Government for working adults.
3. Improve on the Affordable Care Act and eliminate out-of-pocket expenses!
4. Pass laws preventing health insurance companies from denying treatment care options from attending physicians.
5. Pass laws restoring a felon's right to vote or stop having them pay taxes!
6. Pass laws prohibiting the carrying of guns, except in your home or to a gun range.
7. Increase the basic pay of all active-duty service members by a minimum of $1000 monthly!
8. Grant Veterans 100% of their base pay for retirement. They served their country; return the obligation!
9. Make impoverished communities a desirable place to live.
10. Ask voters what they need instead of telling them what you will give them.
11. End police brutality perpetrated against African Americans.
12. End medical care restrictions/pharmacy copays
13. Increase government funding for social welfare programs and create programs to help people overcome living in poverty.

14. Employ HUD and Education Secretaries who want the job and execute their duties to make education and housing a better place to live.

In closing, I want to say everyone's pain should be "everyone's problem." People living in poverty shouldn't have to suffer in a country as great as America. 34 million and climbing are living in poverty in America. How in the "you know what" did this happen? Why is it still a problem? The Bible quotes Jesus saying, "...For ye have the poor always with you;..." (Matthew 26:11-KJV abbreviated passage).

But it also says this, "We then that are **strong** ought to **bear the infirmities** of **the weak**, and not to please ourselves." (Romans 15:1-KJV). I believe the **strong** in this country have been pleasing themselves for too long. Now the time has come for them to give back. What Politicians are doing today is not enough. The numbers don't lie-34 million. What is our government doing behind closed doors?

References

References
Preface

1. Jessica Semega, Melissa Kollar, Emily A Shrider, and John Creamer, "Income, Poverty in the United States: 2019", United Census Bureau, 9/15/2020, (https://www.census.gov/library/publications/2020/demo/p60-270.html.)
2. Tami Luhby, "Biden is about to send $1 billion more in food stamps to the 25 million neediest Americans, CNN.com, 4/2/2021, (https://www.cnn.com/2021/04/02/politics/food-stamps-hunger-americans-relief/index.html).

Chapter 1

3. Leahasilver, "Social Class in America," WordPress, 7/21/2011, (https://leahasilver.wordpress.com) United States Census Bureau, "Income, Poverty and Health Insurance Coverage in the United States: 2019", September 15, 2020, (https://www.census.gov/newsroom/press-releases/2020/income-poverty.html).
4. Mehrabi, Emma, "Poverty in the U.S. will reach drastic levels because of Covid-19", Children's defense fund, 4/21/2020, (https://www.childrensdefense.org/blog/poverty-in-the-u-s-will-reach-drastic-levels-because-of-covid-19/?gclid=Cj0KCQjwyZmEBhCpARIsALIzmnINxR6L03oF8QjnfDZtHV4gp5k-esu_dRG1DYOm9WmSRyLQMNZZjSsaAnmiEALw_wcB.)
5. (8.3 Social Class in the United States", Sociology, University of Minnesota, (https://open.lib.umn.edu/sociology/chapter/8-3-social-class-in-the-united-states/).
6. "U.S. Poverty Statistics," Federal Safety Net, (http://federalsafetynet.com/us-poverty-statistics.html/).

7. Sauter, Michael, "The Face of Poverty," 24/7 Wallst, 1 November 2020, (https://247wallst.com/special-report/2018/09/28/faces-of-poverty/).
8. Jeffrey, Terence P., "List of 80+ Federal Welfare Program", Single Mother Guide, Updated 16 February 2020, (https://singlemotherguide.com/federal-welfare-programs/).

Chapter 2

9. George Friedman, "How Important Is the US President-or Any Leader?", FPF| Geopolitical Futures, 10 November 2016, (https://geopoliticalfutures.com/how-important-is-the-us-president-or-any-leader/)
10. Roody, David Rooy, "15 Timeless Presidential Quotes on Leadership for Presidents Day" Inc., 19 February 2018, (https://www.inc.com/david-van-rooy/15-timeless-presidential-quotes-for-presidents-day.html)
11. Weinstein, Bruce, "What's the Difference Between Compliance and Ethics?", Forbes, 9 May 2019, (https://www.forbes.com/sites/bruceweinstein/2019/05/09/whats-the-difference-between-compliance-and-ethics/#38c540ef7524).
12. Myers, Winslow, "Regardless of party, what we need in a president," Times Herald, 12 July 2018, (https://www.thetimesherald.com/story/opinion/columnists/2018/07/12/regardless-party-need-president/36809789/).

Chapter 3

13. FlowerofScotland, Glasgow, Other, "YouAreAProductOfYourEnvironment" teenink.com, 11/8/2015, https://www.teenink.com/opinion/social_issues_civics/article/838629/You-Are-A-Product-Of-Your-Environment. Assessed on 10/16/2021.
14. (Hedges, Chris, "Recalled to Life," Harig, Amanda, Quora, 25 February 2015, (https://www.quora.com/What-is-the-biggest-slum-in-the-U-S-and-why).
15. (Baker, Kevin, "The First Slum in America," The New York Times, 30 September 2001, https://www.nytimes.com/2001/09/30/books/the-first-slum-in-america.html).
16. America's Drug Overdose Epidemic: Data to Action," Center for Disease Control and Prevention, (https://www.cdc.gov/injury/features/prescription-drug-overdose/index.html)

17. (King, Noel, "Why Is The Opioid Epidemic Overwhelmingly White?", NPR, 4 November 2017, (https://www.npr.org/2017/11/04/562137082/why-is-the-opioid-epidemic-overwhelmingly-white).
18. (https://en.wikipedia.org/wiki/List_of_mass_shootings_in_the_United_States)
19. "Okeefe, Ed and Grace Segers "Biden announces executive actions to curb gun violence "epidemic," 4 April 2021, CBSnews.com, (https://www.cbsnews.com/news/biden-gun-control-executive-actions-violence-epidemic/)
20. Will, Madeline, "To Make Ends Meet, 1 in 5 Teachers Have Second Jobs." Edweek.org, 6/19/ 2018, www.edweek.org/leadership/to-make-ends-meet-1-in-5-teachers-have-second-jobs/2018/06. Assessed 9/25/2021.
21. Taylor, Kelley, "Poverty's Long-List Effects on Students' Education and Success," insightintodiversity.org, 5/30/2017, www.insightintodiversity.com/povertys-long-lasting-effects-on-students-education-and-success. Assessed on 9/25/2021.
22. Klein, Alyson, "No Child Left Behind: An Overview," Education Week, 10 April 2015, (https://www.edweek.org/ew/section/multimedia/no-child-left-behind-overview-definition-summary.html)
23. Camera, Lauren, "No Child Left Behind Has Finally Been Left Behind," usnews.com, 9 December 2015, (https://www.usnews.com/news/articles/2015/12/09/congress-replaces-no-child-left-behind-shifts-power-to-states)
24. Camera, Lauren, "In Most States, Poorest School Districts Get Less Funding," U.S.News.com, 27 February 2018, (https://www.usnews.com/news/best-states/articles/2018-02-27/in-most-states-poorest-school-districts-get-less-funding).
25. Parrett, William and Budge, Kathleen, "What Can Schools Do to Address Poverty?" Edutopia, 10 December 2015, (https://www.edutopia.org/blog/what-can-schools-do-to-address-poverty-william-parrett-kathleen-budge)
26. Federal Emergency Management Agency (FEMA) to step in" "Flint Water Crisis Fast Facts," 790 KABC, 22 April 2016, (https://www.kabc.com/2016/04/22/flint-water-crisis-fast-facts/)
27. Vesoulis, Abby, "Coronavirus May Disproportionately Hurt the Poor-And That's Bad for Everyone," Time.com, 3/11/2020, (https://time.com/5800930/how-coronavirus-will-hurt-the-poor/.)
28. Amadeo, Kimberly| Scott, Gordon [Reviewer], "Federal Poverty Level Guidelines and Chart," The Balance, 7 February 2020, (https://www.

thebalance.com/federal-poverty-level-definition-guidelines-chart-3305843#2020federal-poverty-guidelines-chart)

Chapter 4

29. Jeffrey, Terence P., "List of 80+ Federal Welfare Program", Single Mother Guide, Updated 16 February 2020, (https://singlemotherguide.com/federal-welfare-programs/)
30. "Understanding SNAP, the Supplemental Nutrition Assistance Program," Feeding America, (https://www.feedingamerica.org/take-action/advocate/federal-hunger-relief-programs/snap).
31. Medicare 1010: How Medicare Words", Hello Medicare, (https://hellomedicare.com/medicare-101/?CustomFMO1=HM000337&CustomTrack2=8884896276&hellomedicare_launch_aug2018&ppc&bing&nonbrand&what%20is%20medicare&gclid=d4711be397c015dc56fc453f78ee459d&gclsrc=3p.ds&msclkid=d4711be397c015dc56fc453f78ee459d&utm_source=|bing&utm_medium=cpc&utm_campaign=ba-uhg-hm-nonbrand-influencers&utm_term=what%20is%20medicare&utm_content=early-medicare).
32. Medicaid "Medicaid," Single Mother Guide, Updated 7 February 2020, (https://singlemotherguide.com/medicaid-health-insurance-for-the-poor/).
33. "Understanding The Affordable Care Act," Medical Billing and Coding, (https://www.medicalbillingandcoding.org/health-insurance-guide/affordable-care-act/).

Chapter 5

34. Jessica Semega, Melissa Kollar, John Creamer, and Abinash Mohanty, "Income and Poverty in the United States: 2018", census.gov, September 2019, (https://www.census.gov/data/tables/2019/demo/income-poverty/p60-266.html).
35. Gonzales, Matt, "Mental Illness and Poverty: A Depressing Reality," The Recovery Village, 9 November 2019, (https://www.therecoveryvillage.com/mental-health/related/mental-illness-and-poverty/).
36. Frederic Michas, "Mental health facilities by type of facility in the U.S. 2019, statista.com, October 20, 2020, https://www.statista.com/statistics/712614/mental-health-facilities-number-in-the-us-by-facility-

type/#:~:text=Mental%20health%20facilities%20are%20critically%20important%20for%20treating,that%20year%20with%20just%20708%20facilities%20in%20total.

37. (https://adaa.org/understanding-anxiety/facts-statistics#:~:text=Facts%20%26%20Statistics.%20Advertisement.%20Anxiety%20disorders%20are%20the,yet%20only%2036.9%25%20of%20those%20suffering%20receive%20treatment.)
38. "The Effects of Poverty," Moveforhunger.org, https://moveforhunger.org/the-effects-of-poverty. Accessed on 10/16/2021.
39. Dolan, Karen, "The Poor Get Prison: The Alarming Spread of the Criminalization of Poverty," Institute for Policy Studies, 18 March 2015, (https://ips-dc.org/the-poor-get-prison-the-alarming-spread-of-the-criminalization-of-poverty/).

Chapter 6

40. https://www.ssa.gov/ssi/text-income-ussi.htm

Chapter 7

41. Andrezejewski, Adam, "New Report: Nearly $300 Billion In Foreign Aid Spent By U.S. Government," forbes.com, 8/4/2021, https://www.forbes.com/sites/adamandrzejewski/2021/08/04/new-report-nearly-300-billion-in-foreign-aid-spent-by-us-government/?sh=2f88f3a34374. Assessed on 10/16/2021.
42. (Gaille, Brandon, "21 Advantages and Disadvantages of Foreign Aid", BrandonGaille, 27 February 2018, (https://brandongaille.com/21-advantages-disadvantages-foreign-aid/).

Chapter 8

43. Fact Sheet: Hunger and Poverty in the Military Community, bread.org, 7/20/2018, https://bread.org/library/fact-sheet-hunger-and-poverty-military-community. Accessed on 10/17/2021.
44. NPR, "Military Families and SNAP Benefits," February 17, 2018, (https://www.npr.org/2018/02/17/586759930/military-families-and-snap-benefits)

45. Lightfoot, Lizann, "How WIC Benefits Military Families," the Military Wallet, 10 April 2019, (https://themilitarywallet.com/wic-benefits-military-families/).

Chapter 9

46. Novotney, Amy, "Stopping military and Veteran suicides" Apa.org, 1/1/2020, www.apa.org/monitor/2020/01/ce-corner-suicide. Accessed 10/2/2021.
47. (Author Unknown, "10 Misconceptions About Suicide").
48. ("2019 National Veteran Suicide Prevention Annual Report" Office of Mental Health and Suicide Prevention, U.S. Department of Veterans Affairs, https://www.mentalhealth.va.gov/docs/data-sheets/2019/2019_National_Veteran_Suicide_Prevention_Annual_Report_508.pdf).

Chapter 10

49. (Nelson, Steven, "Trump signs three executive orders taking aims at unions," Washington Examiner, 25 May 2018, https://www.washingtonexaminer.com/news/white-house/trump-guts-union-perks-speeds-up-civil-service-firings-to-save-100-million-a-year.)

Chapter 11

50. Taylor, Jim, Ph.D., "Six Reasons Why Politicians Believe They Can Lie," Psychology Today, 24 September 2012, (https://www.psychologytoday.com/us/blog/the-power-prime/201209/six-reasons-why-politicians-believe-they-can-lie#:~:text=Ultimately,%20politicians%20lie%20because,%20due,to%20indefensible%20claims%20against%20them).
51. Savitsky, Shane, "The perks of being a member of Congress" AXIOS, 28 November 2017, (https://www.axios.com/the-perks-of-being-a-member-of-congress-1513307200-ba8cb415-27c0-4ee9-ac1f-f445d175bf68.html).
52. Gabriel, Brian, "Types of Democrats," theclassroom.com, 5/10/2019, theclassroom.com/types-democrats-11944.html. Assessed on 10/2/2021.

www.ingramcontent.com/pod-product-compliance
Lightning Source LLC
Chambersburg PA
CBHW031023190726
48286CB00003BA/983

* 9 7 8 1 9 5 7 5 8 2 6 5 8 *